The Preacher's Homiletic Helper

The Preacher's Homiletic Helper

Algerton C. P. Coote

BAKER BOOK HOUSE
Grand Rapids, Michigan

Formerly published
under the title,
Bible Helps for Busy Men
Reprinted 1975 by
Baker Book House
ISBN: 0-8010-2368-8

PHOTOLITHOPRINTED BY CUSHING - MALLOY, INC.
ANN ARBOR, MICHIGAN, UNITED STATES OF AMERICA
1975

INTRODUCTION.

THIS book does not profess, in any sense, to be exhaustive; but is rather, as its title implies, suggestive of further study.

The Scripture-subjects have been copied from notes, made during the past few years in an interleaved Bible.

They are now published, at the special request of several friends, in the hope that, while the price of the book will bring it within the reach of all, the matter contained in its pages may prove some little help to "Busy Men."

A. C. P. C.

CONTENTS.

"A little reviving"	21
"A threefold cord"	15
Able, God is, We are not	22
Abundant entrance, An	34
Affinity, Effect of ungodly	23
"Anything"	58
Arm of the Lord, The	50
"Armour of God, The whole"	65
Assurance of Salvation	7
"At the Feet of Jesus"	97
"At hand"	39
Backsliding	83
Be—Be not	75
Beauty	94
Before His people, &c.	30
Benedictions (New Testament)	94
Blood of Jesus, The	8
"Books opened, The"	17
Born of God	96
"Bruised for our iniquities"	98
By "His own Blood"	8
Called—Calling	43
Calls, Double	62
Captains of tribes	99
Cares (anxious thoughts)	104
Carry	50
Characteristics of children of God, &c. (Epistles of John)	36
"Children, Little" (1 John)	69
Children of God, to be filled with	44
Children, or sons of God	44
Children, Thoughts about	78, 79
Christ, The Deity of	77
Christ, In, of, as (Ephesians)	64
Christ, Second coming of	101
"Christ, The" (in Corinthians)	63
Christian homes (Acts)	61
Christian, Why am I a?	66
Cities of refuge	86
"Clean"	86
Cleanseth, He	87
Clouds (Job xxxvi. xxxvii.)	51
Come	52
"Come unto Me"	52
Comfort (Isaiah)	46
Coming of the Lord	101
Commands and invitations	84
Commands, God's	90, 92
Conditional promises	72
Confidence	43
Continually (1 Chron. xvi.)	9
Continue	53
Cross, Title on the	84

	PAGE		PAGE
Crowns, Three	21	"Feet, At Jesus'"	97
"Cursed" (Jeremiah)	46	Following the Lord	68
		For the sake	48
Daniel, a representation of the Lord	90	Forty days and forty nights	96
		"Foundation of the world"	13
David's downward, and upward steps	28	Fountain, The Lord a	32
		Four privileges	35
Deity of Christ, The	77	Four steps in one day	27
Devil-possessed man, The	23	Four more steps (Luke v.)	27
Direction, Divine	74	"From whence cometh my help?"	99
Do you want? ("in Him")	9		
Doing righteousness	52		
Double calls	62	**Gifts, from and to God**	1
		Gifts of God (John)	77
Eagle, The	45	Gifts of New Covenant (Jer. xxxi.)	76
Early-rising, Instances of	24	Give thanks, Who may?	98
Effect of Ungodly affinity	23	Giving, Examples of	69
Elihu's speech, "Clouds"	51	"Glorious" things (in Epistles)	62
Emmanuel	89	God, Born of	96
"Entrance abundantly, An"	34	God (Light, Love, Life)	97
Enquiry-room texts	66	God of, The	31
"Eternal Life"	85	"God, In" (Ps. lxii. 7)	100
"Even as"	74	God is able, We not able	22
"Everlasting" (Isaiah)	29	God is Our (Psalms)	30
"Everlasting punishment"	40	God seeks	61
Examples of giving	69	God the Rock	20
"Exceeding"	33	God, The whole armour of	65
Excellent, The Lord is	30	God, The will of	73, 74
Eyes of the Lord, The	19	"God with us," We with God	89
Ezra's genealogy	89	Godly servants	87
		God's commands	90, 92
Faith (practical)	10	God's Unanswered questions	71
Faith, Promises to (Rom. v. 1, 2)	35	Gospel, The	69
Faith: What it receives	10	Grace, and Glory (the Gospel of)	62
Faith's possibilities	11	Grace and works	37–39
Faith's privileges	11	"Great" things (Seven)	17
"Faithful" men	88	"Great things" of the Lord	17
Faithful, Promises to the	88		
"Faithful saying"s	88	**Hath—Will (Psalms)**	29
"Father"	56	He and me	81
Fear of the Lord, The	85	He cleanseth	87

Contents.

	PAGE		PAGE
"He was bruised"	98	Kneeling in prayer	60
Healer, The (Jehovah-Rophi)	25	Know, We (1 John)	54
Heart of the Lord, The	93	Knoweth, The Lord	90
Heart, With the whole (Ps. cxix.)	43		
Help, From whence cometh?	99	"Lay hold"	34
"Henceforth" (in New Test.)	58	Leader, The Lord a (Isaiah)	31
Hide, Hiding-place	49	Learn	83
"His Love"	35	Liberty	59
"His own Blood, By"	8	"Life, Eternal"	85
"His Steps"	26	Limiting Christ's Power (John xi.)	18
His Voice	103	"Little children" (1 John)	69
"Hold fast"	34	Lot's downward, and upward steps	27
Homes, Christian (Acts)	61	"Love, His"	35
Households, God's commands to	92	Love of Christ, The	3
Humility	82	Love of God, The	2
		Love to God, Shewn by keeping His commandments	90
"I am with thee"	19		
"I will be with thee"	19		
"I will not"	84	"Master, The"	76
"If any man" (John)	97	"Me, With"	95
In Christ, of Christ, as Christ (Ephesians)	64	Meaning of names of twelve captains of tribes	99
"In God" (Ps. lxii. 7)	100	"Must"	101
"In the Lord" (Isa. xlv.)	26	"My God," Those who said	91
"In the midst," Jesus	35		
"In the midst," "Out of the midst" (Zeph. iii.)	34	Name of the Lord, The	12, 13
Increase	47	Names of twelve captains of tribes	99
Invitations and commands	84	Nazareth, Jesus of	95
"It is finished"	84	"Needy, Poor and"	44
		New Covenant, Gifts of (Jer. xxxi.)	76
Jehovah	25	Now	72
Jehovah-Jireh (the Provider)	26		
Jehovah-Rophi (the Healer)	25	Obedience, Results of	18
Jesus, At the Feet of	97	"One thing"	97
Jesus, The Blood of	8	Only	47
Jesus, Daniel representation of	90	"Opened, The Books"	17
Jesus of Nazareth	95	Our Lord's Petitions (John xvii.)	60
Jesus in the midst	35	"Out of the midst," "In the midst" (Zeph. iii.)	43
Jordan, When you have crossed	93		

Contents.

	PAGE
Partakers	33
"Peace, Peace"	18
Peter's downward, and upward steps	28
Petitions, Our Lord's (John xvii.)	60
Pleasures: A contrast	17
"Poor and needy"	44
Prayer and praise (together)	29
Prayer, Kneeling in	60
Prayer, Success in	58
Preparation	100
Privileges, Four	35
Promises, Unconditional and conditional	72
Promises to faith (Rom. v. 1, 2)	35
Promises to the faithful	88
Promises to the upright	91
Promises to "waiting"	103
Promises, Three (Phil. iv.)	49
Provider, The (Jehovah-Jireh)	26
"Punishment, Everlasting"	40
Questions, God's Unanswered	71
Quiet, Quieted, Quietly, Quietness	51
Ready	87
Redemption	80, 81
Refuge, Cities of	86
Rejoice	55
Results of obedience	18
Reviving	21
Righteousness, Doing	52
Rock, God the	20
"Sacrifices of thanksgiving"	98
Safe, Safety, Safely	67
Sake, For the	48
Salvation, Assurance of	7
Salvation, Full, Present, Free	5, 6
Sanctification—Sanctify	14

	PAGE
Satisfaction: A contrast	32
Second coming of the Lord	101
Seek, We are to, We are not to	57
Seeking and finding	56
Seeks, God	61
Servants, Godly	87
Seven "Great" things	17
Seven "Without"s	63
Shade, Shadow	49
Shepherd, The	40
Sin, Consequences of, What is sin? How removed? Victory over sin	15, 16
Sins of God's people	16
Sincerity	62
Snow, White as	94
Sons, or children, of God	44
"Spirit of, The" (Romans)	63
Spiritualism	40
"Stand still"	23
Steps, "His Steps"	26
Steps, Four in one day; Four more (Luke v.)	27
Steps, downward and upward, Lot's, David's, Peter's	27, 28
Substitution	4
Success in prayer	58
Texts, Enquiry-room	66
Thanks, Who may give?	98
"Thanksgiving, Sacrifices of"	98
"The Christ" (in Corinthians)	63
The Gospel	62, 69
The Lord a Fountain	32
The Lord a Leader (Isaiah)	31
The Lord, The Arm of	50
The Lord before His people, &c.	30
The Lord is excellent	30
The Lord, The Heart of	93
The Lord knoweth	90
The Lord, Second coming of	101

Contents.

	PAGE		PAGE
The way	53	We are not able, God is able	22
The world	70, 71	We know (1 John)	54
Those who said "my God"	91	Weights	67
Three crowns	21	"Well-pleased," "Well-pleasing"	96
"Threefold cord, A"	15	"What is Truth?"	59
Title on the Cross, The	84	"Whatsoever"	42
Treasure	48	When you have crossed Jordan	93
Tribes, Names of twelve captains of	99	Where the Lord is	30
		White as snow	94
"Trust" (Proverbs)	45	Who may give thanks?	98
"Truth, What is?"	59	Whole armour of God, The	65
		Whole heart, With the (Ps. cxix.)	43
Unanswered questions, God's	71	"Whosoever," "Whatsoever"	41, 42
Unconditional promises	72	Why am I a Christian?	66
Ungodly affinity, Effect of	23	Will of God, The	73, 74
"Until"	46	Wings, His	23
Upright, Promises to the	91	"With Me"	95
		"With us, God", We with God	89
Victory over sin	16	"Without" (Hebrews)	63
Voice, His	103	"Without"s, Seven	63
		Works, and Grace	37–39
Waiting	102	World, The	70, 71
"Waiting," Promises to	103		
Walk	21	**"Ye are not come, but ye are come" (Heb. xii.)**	65
Watch	65		
Way, The	53	"Yet a little while"	45
"STONES ROLLED AWAY"			105

GIFTS FROM GOD.

"His only begotten Son;" "Himself"	John 3. 16, with Tit. 2. 14.
"How shall He not with Him also freely give us all things?"	Rom. 8. 32.
The Holy Spirit	Luke 11. 13; John 14. 16.
A new heart	Ezek. 36. 26.
Power (the right) to be His sons	John 1. 12.
Repentance	Acts 5. 31.
Forgiveness of sins	Acts 5. 31.
Faith	Eph. 2. 8.
Eternal life	Rom. 6. 23; John 10. 28.
Peace	John 14. 27.
Rest	Matt. 11. 28.
Strength	Ps. 29. 11; Isa. 40. 29.
His word	John 17. 14.
Desires of the heart	Ps. 37. 4.
A crown of life	Rev. 2. 10.
Grace and glory	Ps. 84. 11.
"Thanks be unto God for His unspeakable Gift"	2 Cor. 9. 15.

GIFTS TO GOD.

"First their own selves"	2 Cor. 8. 5.
The heart	Prov. 23. 25.
Our love	Song of Sol. 7. 12.
Thanks	Ps. 30. 12; 1 Thess. 5. 18.
Fruit of our lips	Heb. 13. 15.
Your bodies	Rom. 12. 1.
As we are able	Deut. 16. 17; Luke 11. 41. (marg.)
Glory and strength	Ps. 96. 7, 8.
"Of Thine own have we given Thee"	1 Chron. 29. 14.

THE LOVE OF GOD.

Yea, I have *loved* thee with an *everlasting love* — Jer. 31. 3.

In this was manifested *the love of God* toward us, because that *God sent* His only-begotten Son into the world, that we might live through Him . . . . 1 John 4. 9.

God *so loved* the world, that *He gave* His only-begotten Son . . . . John iii. 16.

God commendeth *His love* toward us, in that, while we were *yet sinners*, Christ died for us — Rom. 5. 8.

God, who is rich in mercy, for *His great love*, wherewith He *loved us*, even when we were *dead in sins*, hath *quickened us together* with Christ, hath *raised us up together*, *and made us sit together* in heavenly places in Christ Jesus . . . . Eph. 2. 4-6.

The *love of God* is shed abroad in our hearts by the Holy Ghost . . . . Rom. 5. 5.

That *the love* wherewith Thou hast *loved me* may be in them . . . . John 17. 26.

I am persuaded that neither death nor life . . . nor any other creature shall be able to separate us from *the love of God* which is in Christ Jesus . . . . Rom. 8. 38, 39.

Behold, what *manner of love* the Father hath bestowed upon us, that we should be called the *sons of God*. . . . Beloved, *now* are we the *sons of God* . . . . 1 John 3. 1, 2.

THE LOVE OF CHRIST.

Walk in love, as Christ also *hath loved us*, and hath given Himself for us . . . Eph. 5. 2.

Unto Him that *loved us*, and washed us from our sins in His own blood . . . Rev. 1. 5.

Greater love hath no man than this, that a man lay down his life for his friends . . John 15. 13; 1 John 3. 16.

Having *loved His own* which were in the world, He loved them unto the end . . . John 13. 1.

As the Father hath *loved Me*, so have *I loved you:* continue ye in *My love* . . . John 15. 9.

And to know *the love of Christ*, which *passeth knowledge* . . . . . Eph. 3. 19.

For *the love of Christ* constraineth us, . . . that if one died for all, then were all dead: and that He died for all, that they which live should not henceforth live unto themselves, but unto Him which died for them, and rose again . . . . . 2 Cor. 5. 14. 15.

The life, which I now live . . . I live, by the faith of *the Son of God, Who loved me*, and gave Himself for me . . . . Gal. 2. 20.

We love Him, because *He first loved us* . . 1 John 4. 19.

SUBSTITUTION.

God will provide Himself a lamb	Gen. 22. 8.
When I see the blood, I will pass over you	Ex. 12, 13, 23.
The goat shall bear all their iniquities	Lev. 16. 22; see also Lev. 1. 4, and 14. 4-7.
A red heifer without spot . . . a purification for sin	Num. 19. 2, 9; Heb. 9. 12-14.
Moses made a serpent of brass, and put it upon a pole	Num. 21. 9; John iii. 14.
Until the death of the high priest (cities of Refuge)	Josh. 20. 6; Heb. 2. 14. 15.
My God, My God, why hast Thou forsaken Me?	Ps. 22. 1; Mark 15. 34.
The Lord hath laid on Him the iniquity of us all	Isa. 53. 6; Acts 8. 32, 35.
Cast me forth . . . so shall the sea be calm unto you	Jonah 1. 12; 2. 3; Matt. 12. 40.

Behold the Lamb of God, that taketh away sin	John 1. 29.
I lay down my life for the sheep	John 10. 15.
Justified freely by His grace, through the redemption in Christ Jesus	Rom. 3. 24.
He hath made Him to be sin for us, who knew no sin	2 Cor. 5. 21.
Christ being made a curse for us	Gal. 3. 13.
Without shedding of blood is no remission	Heb. 9. 22; Lev. 17. 11.
To put away sin by the sacrifice of Himself	Heb. 9. 26: 10. 10
Redeemed with the precious blood of Christ, &c.	1 Peter 1. 18, 19
Who His own self bare our sins in His own body on the tree, &c.	1 Peter 2. 24.
The just for the unjust, that He might bring us to God	1 Peter 3. 18.
The blood of Jesus Christ His Son cleanseth us from all sin*	1 John 1. 7.
The propitiation for our sins	1 John 2. 2; 4. 10.
Unto Him that loved us, and washed us from our sins in His own blood	Rev. 1. 5.

* For other passages about "the Blood" see page 8.

SALVATION:

"FULL, PRESENT, AND FREE."

FULL.

The grace of God bringeth salvation to all men	Titus 2. 11.
He is the author of eternal salvation	Heb. 5. 9.
He is mighty to save	Isa. 63. 1.
Able to save to the uttermost	Heb. 7. 25.
Christ Jesus came to save sinners	1 Tim. 1. 15.
Come to seek, and to save the lost	Luke 19. 10.
Him that cometh in nowise cast out	John 6. 37.
Whosoever believeth shall not perish	John 3. 16.
Blood of Jesus . . . cleanseth from all sin	1 John 1. 7.
Though sins as scarlet . . . as white as snow	Isa. 1. 18.
All sins cast into depths of the sea	Micah 7. 19.
Sins blotted out as a thick cloud	Isa. 44. 22.
Sins removed as far as east from west	Ps. 103. 12.
Sins remembered no more	Heb. 10. 17.
He shall save His people from their sins	Matt. 1. 21.
He redeems us from all iniquity	Titus 2. 14.
Christ manifested to destroy the works of the devil	1 John 3. 8.
We are saved from wrath through Him	Rom. 5. 9.
We have peace with God through Him	Rom. 5.1; John 14.27.
He gives us rest	Matt. 11. 28.
He gives us power	John 1. 12; Isa. 40. 29.
He gives life, and life more abundantly	John 10. 10.
We may always triumph in Christ	2 Cor. 2. 14.
All grace abounds toward us	2 Cor. 9. 8.
We shall (if His sheep) never perish; no one can pluck us out of His hand	John 10. 28.
Kept by the power of God, through faith unto salvation	1 Peter 1. 5.

SALVATION—*continued.*

PRESENT.

Come NOW, and let us reason together	Isa. 1. 18.
Behold, NOW is the accepted time, NOW is the day of salvation	2 Cor. 6. 2.
There is therefore NOW no condemnation	Rom. 8. 1.
He that believeth HATH everlasting life	John 5. 24; 6. 47; 1 John 5. 12.
He IS passed from death unto life	John 5. 24.
Little children, your sins ARE forgiven	1 John 2. 12.
We HAVE redemption through His blood	Eph. 1. 7; Col. 1. 13. 14.
He HATH quickened and raised us up together with Christ	Eph. 2. 5, 6.
By one offering He HATH perfected for ever	Heb. 10. 14.
TO-DAY shalt thou be with Me in paradise	Luke 23. 43.
THIS DAY is salvation come	Luke 19. 9.
Beloved, NOW are we the sons of God	1 John 3. 2.

FREE.

It is the GIFT of God . . . not of works	Eph. 2. 8, 9; Rom 4. 5.
The FREE GIFT came upon all unto justification	Rom. 5. 18.
The GIFT of God is eternal life	Rom. 6. 23; 1 John 5. 11.
Jesus . . . GIVES repentance and forgiveness of sins	Acts 5. 31.
My peace I GIVE unto you *	John 14. 27.
Come WITHOUT MONEY and without price	Isa. 55. 1.
Whosoever WILL, let him take of the water of life FREELY	Rev. 22. 17.

Salvation is of the Lord	Jonah 2. 9.
Neither is there salvation in any other	Acts 4. 12.
Believe on the Lord Jesus Christ, and *thou* shalt be saved	Acts 16. 31; Prov. 22. 19.

Now is our salvation nearer than when we believed	Rom. 13. 11; 1 Peter 1. 5.

* See "GIFTS from God," page 1.

ASSURANCE OF SALVATION.

To give *knowledge* of salvation	Luke 1. 77.
I know My sheep, and *am known* of Mine	John 10. 14.
Ye (that believe) may *know* that ye have eternal life	1 John 5. 13.
I *know* whom I have believed	2 Tim. 1. 12.
We *know* that we are of God	1 John 5. 19; 3. 14.
I am *persuaded*, that neither life, nor death . . . shall be able to separate us from the love of God	Rom. 8. 38, 39.
The Lord is *my* Shepherd, I shall not want	Ps. 23. 1.
God is *my* salvation; I will trust, and not be afraid	Isa. 12. 2; Hab. 3. 17, 18.
My Beloved is *mine*, and *I am His*	Song of Sol. 2. 16.
The Lord *shall deliver me* from every evil work, *and will preserve me* unto His heavenly kingdom	2 Tim. 4. 18.
The Spirit beareth witness with our spirit, that *we are* the children of God	Rom. 8. 16.
He that believeth *hath* the witness in himself	1 John 5. 10.
Let us draw near, in *full assurance* of faith	Heb. 10. 22.
Show the same diligence, to the *full assurance* of hope unto the end	Heb. 6. 11.
I *know* that my Redeemer liveth	Job 19. 25.
For He hath said, I will NEVER leave thee, nor forsake thee	Heb. 13. 5.

THE BLOOD OF JESUS CHRIST.

By it we obtain—

Atonement	Lev. 17. 11; 16. 15, 16; Rom. 5. 11.
Our purchase	Acts 20. 28.
Redemption	Eph. 1. 7; Col. 1. 14.
Justification	Rom. 3. 24, 25; 5. 9.
The (new) covenant	Heb. 9. 20; 13. 20.
Remission of sins	Matt. 26. 28; Heb. 9. 22.
Life	Gen. 9. 4; John 6. 53, 54.
Peace	Col. 1. 20; Rom. 5, 1, 9.
Sprinkling	Heb. 12. 24; 1 Pet. 1. 2.
Sanctification	Heb. 10. 29; 13. 12.
Conscience (purged)	Heb. 9. 14.
Washing	Rev. 1. 5.
Cleansing	1 John 1. 7.
Boldness of access	Heb. 10. 19.
Nearness	Eph. 2. 13.
Communion	1 Cor. 10. 16.
Sustenance	John 6. 55.
Abiding	John 6. 56.
Whiteness (purity)	Rev. 7. 14.
Victory	Rev. 12. 11.
"When I see the blood, I will pass over you"	Ex. 12. 13, 23; with Heb. 9. 22.

BY "HIS OWN BLOOD."

He purchased the Church	Acts 20, 28.
He entered into the holy place	Heb. 9. 12; with 10. 19.
He obtained eternal redemption for us	Heb. 9. 12.
He sanctified the people	Heb. 13. 12.
He washed us from our sins	Rev. 1. 5.

DO YOU WANT?

Life	in Him	John 1. 4.
Salvation	in the Lord	Isa. 45. 17.
Forgiveness	in Whom	Eph. 1. 7; Col. 1. 14.
Acceptance	in the Beloved	Eph. 1. 6.
Righteousness	in Christ Jesus	1 Cor. 1. 30.
Peace	in Me	John 16. 33.
Rest	in the Lord	Ps. 37. 7.
Joy	in the Lord	Habak. 3. 18.
Help	in Me	Hosea 13. 9.
Strength	in the Lord	Eph. 6. 10.
Victory	in Christ	2 Cor. 2. 14.
Preservation	in Jesus Christ	Jude 1.
Wisdom and knowledge	in Whom	Col. 2. 3.
Boldness and access	in Whom	Eph. 3. 12.
Answers to prayer	in Me	John 15. 7.
Sanctification	in Christ Jesus	1 Cor. 1. 30.
To be fruitful	in Me	John 15. 5.
To do all things	in Christ (Gr.)	Phil. 4. 13.
All need supplied	in Christ (Gr.)	Phil. 4. 19.
All spiritual blessings	in Christ	Eph. 1. 3.
An inheritance	in Whom	Eph. 1. 11.
Confidence at His coming	in Him	1 John 2. 28.
Ye are COMPLETE	IN HIM	Col. 2. 10; with 1. 28 (end).

"CONTINUALLY."

1 CHRON. 16.

Continual song	1 Chron. 16. 6.
Continual seeking	1 Chron. 16. 11.
Continual service	1 Chron. 16. 37.
Continual sacrifice	1 Chron. 16. 40.

FAITH (PRACTICAL).

FORSAKING
Let the wicked *forsake* his way, and the unrighteous man his thoughts: and let him return unto the Lord, and He will have mercy upon him: and to our God, for He will abundantly pardon . . Isa. 55. 7.

ALL,
I count *all* things but loss, for the excellency of the knowledge of Christ Jesus my Lord: for whom I have suffered the loss of *all* things, and do count them but dung, that I may win Christ . . Phil. 3. 8.

I
I am crucified with Christ: nevertheless I live; yet *not I*, but *Christ liveth in me:* and the life which I now live in the flesh, I live by the faith of the Son of God, Who loved me, and gave Himself for me . Gal. 2. 20.

TAKE
Take My yoke upon you, and learn of Me; for I am meek and lowly in heart: and ye shall find rest unto your souls . . Matt. 11. 29.

HIM.
My Beloved is mine, and I am His . . Song of Sol. 2. 16.
We are in *Him* that is true, even in His Son Jesus Christ . . . . 1 John 5. 20.

WHAT FAITH RECEIVES.

"WITH GOD ALL THINGS ARE POSSIBLE."

Justification	. Rom. 5. 1; Gal. 2. 16.
Remission of sins . . .	. Acts 10. 43.
A purified heart . . .	. Acts 15. 9.
Sanctification	. Acts 26. 18.
Everlasting life	. John 3. 16; 6. 47.
Adoption as children of light . .	. John 12. 36.
The promised Spirit . . .	. Gal. 3. 14.
Standing	. 2 Cor. 1. 24.
Righteousness	. Rom. 3. 22; Phil. 3. 9.

FAITH'S PRIVILEGES.
"ALL THINGS ARE YOURS."

Christ dwelling in your hearts	Eph. 3. 17.
Boldness and access with confidence	Eph. 3. 12.
Full assurance	Heb. 10. 22.
All joy and peace	Rom. 15. 13.
Perfect peace	Isa. 26. 3.
A fixed heart	Ps. 112. 7.
Everlasting strength	Isa. 26. 4.
Never to thirst	John 6. 35.
Not to abide in darkness	John 12. 46.
Not to be left desolate	Ps. 34. 22.
Not to be troubled	John 14. 1.
Not to be ashamed	Rom. 9. 33.
Not to make haste	Isa. 28. 16.
Not to be afraid of evil tidings	Ps. 112. 7.
Cannot be removed	Ps. 125. 1.
Shall never die	John 11. 26.
Kept unto salvation	1 Peter 1. 5.

FAITH'S POSSIBILITIES.
"ALL THINGS ARE POSSIBLE TO HIM THAT BELIEVETH."

To live Christ	Gal. 2. 20; Heb. 10. 38.
To stand fast	1 Cor. 16. 13.
To walk	2 Cor. 5. 7.
Christian unity	Acts 4. 32.
Through prayer to save the sick	James 5. 15.
To obtain all things, whatsoever we ask	Matt. 21. 22; Mark 11. 23, 24.
Victory over the world	1 John 5. 4.
To quench all the fiery darts of the wicked	Eph. 6. 16.
To work righteousness, to obtain promises	Heb. 11. 33.
To overflow with the Spirit towards others	John 7. 38.
To do the works of Christ, and even greater	John 14. 12.
To inherit the promises	Heb. 6. 12.

"Whatsoever is not of faith is sin."
"Without faith it is impossible to please Him."

THE NAME OF THE LORD.
(MATT. 1. 21.)

Is as ointment poured forth	Song of Sol. 1. 3.
Is excellent	Ps. 8. 1, 9.
Is holy and reverend	Ps. 111. 9; Matt. 6. 9.
Is to be sanctified	Isa. 29. 23.
Is to be praised	Ps. 113. 3.
Is to be declared	Ps. 22. 22; Rom. 15. 9.
None other name given for salvation	Acts 4. 12.
A strong tower for the righteous	Prov. 18. 10.

We have—
- Life through His name — John 20. 31.
- Remission of sins through His name — Acts 10. 43.
- Washing in His name — 1 Cor. 6. 11.
- Sanctification in His name — 1 Cor. 6. 11.
- Justification in His name — 1 Cor. 6. 11.
- Prayer answered in His name — John 14. 13.
- Devils cast out in His name — Mark 16. 17; Luke 10. 17; Acts 16. 18.
- Holy Ghost sent in His name — John 14. 26.

Prayers in, or for His name—
- Pardon mine iniquity, for Thy name's sake — Ps. 25. 11.
- Quicken me, for Thy name's sake — Ps. 143. 11.
- Guide me, for Thy name's sake — Ps. 31. 3; 23. 3.
- Help me, for the glory of Thy name — Ps. 79. 9.
- Unite my heart to fear Thy name — Ps. 86. 11.

We are to—
- Know His name — Ps. 9. 10.
- Give glory to His name — Ps. 29. 2; 1 Chron. 16. 29.
- Call upon His name — Ps. 105. 1.
- Love His name — Ps. 5. 11; 69. 36.
- Think upon His name — Mal. 3. 16.
- Believe in His name — John 1. 12. Acts 3. 16.
- Trust in His name — Zeph. 3. 12; Matt. 12. 21.
- Fear His name — Mal. 4. 2.
- Walk up and down in His name — Zech. 10. 12; Mic. 4. 5.
- Make mention of His name only — Isa. 26. 13.
- Preach in His name — Acts 9. 27.

THE NAME OF THE LORD
(continued).

We are to—

Give thanks in His name	Eph. 5. 20.
Give a cup of water in His name	Mark 9. 41.
Receive a child in His name	Matt. 18. 5.
Suffer for His name	Acts 5.41; Matt.10.22.
Be reproached for His name	1 Peter 4. 14.
Labour for His name	Heb. 6. 10; Rev. 2. 3.
Hold fast His name	Rev. 2. 13.
Not deny His name	Rev. 3. 8.
Do all in His name	Col. 3. 17.
Gather together in His name	Matt. 18. 20; 1 Cor. 5. 4.

We are—

A people taken out for His name	Acts 15. 14.
Chosen to bear His name	Acts 9. 15.
Baptized into His name	Acts 19. 5.

His name endures for ever	Ps. 72. 17, 19.
Every knee shall bow to it	Phil. 2. 10; Isa. 45. 23.
His name shall be in their foreheads	Rev. 22. 4; with Rev. 3. 12.
BLESS HIS NAME	Ps. 100. 4.

Let every one, that nameth the name of Christ, depart from iniquity . . . . 2 Tim. 2. 19.

"FROM (OR BEFORE) THE FOUNDATION OF THE WORLD."

Kingdom	prepared	Matt. 25. 34.
Blood of prophets	shed	Luke 11. 50.
Christ	loved	John 17. 24.
In Him	chosen	Eph. 1. 4.
The works	finished	Heb. 4. 3.
Christ	Foreordained	1 Peter 1. 20.
The Lamb	slain	Rev. 13. 8.
Book of	life	Rev. 17. 8.

SANCTIFICATION—SANCTIFY.
(First mention in Bible, Gen. 2, 3.)

The Hebrew word in the Old Test., and the corresponding Greek word in the New Test., are also translated as follows:

The *Substantive*—
"Sanctuary;" "holiness;" "sanctification;" "saints."

The *Verb*, &c.—

"Hallowed,"	frequently	Ex. 29. 21 (1st time).
"Holy," "Most holy,"	frequently	Ex. 3. 5 (1st time).
"Dedicate, ed,"	ten times	Judges 17.3(1st time).
"Consecrate, ed,"	seven times	Ex.28.3; 30.30; Josh 6.19; 2Chron.26.18; 29.33;31.6; Ezra 3.5.
"Prepare,"	seven times (always in connection with war, or punishment)	Jer. 6. 4;-12.3; 22. 7; 51. 27, 28; Joel 3. 9. Micah 3. 5.
"Defiled,"	once	Deut. 22. 9.
"Appointed,"	once	Josh. 20. 7.
"Purified,"	once	2 Sam. 11. 4.
"Proclaim,"	once	2 Kings 10. 20.
"Kept,"	once	Isa. 30. 29.
"Bid,"	once	Zeph. 1. 7.

Only one rendering in English could be substituted in each place; namely, "separate, ed," or "set apart."

SEE EZEK. 20. 12 (end).

For our sakes Christ sanctified Himself	John 17. 19.
He is our Sanctification	1 Cor. 1. 30.

We are—

To be saints—sanctified ones	1 Cor. 1. 2; Isa. 13. 3.
To sanctify the Lord in our hearts	1 Pet. 3. 15; Isa. 8. 13.

We are sanctified by—

The Father	John 10. 36; Jude 1.
The Son (Gr.)	1 Cor. 1. 2.
The Holy Ghost	Rom. 15. 16; 1 Cor. 6. 11.
The offering of Jesus	Heb. 10. 14; 13. 12.
The name of Jesus	1 Cor. 6. 11.
The will of God	Heb. 10. 10; 1 Thess. 4. 3.
The word (truth)	John 17.17; 1 Tim.4.5.
Prayer	1 Tim. 4. 5.
Faith in Christ	Acts 26. 18; see also 1 Cor. 7. 14.

"The very God of peace sanctify you wholly" . 1 Thess. 5. 53.

"A THREEFOLD CORD."

God so LOVED THE WORLD, that He gave His only-begotten Son, that whosoever believeth in Him should not perish, but have everlasting life . . . . . John 3. 16.

Herein is love, not that we loved God, but that He LOVED US, and sent His Son to be the propitiation for our sins . . . 1 John 4. 10.

The life, which I now live in the flesh, I live by the faith of the Son of God, Who LOVED ME, and gave Himself for me . . . Gal. 2. 20.

"GOD IS LOVE."

SIN, AND ITS CONSEQUENCES.

By one man sin entered into the world . . Rom. 5. 12.
We are conceived in sin . . . . Ps. 51. 5.
All have sinned, and come short . . . Rom. 3. 23; Gal. 3. 22.
Every man shall be put to death for his own sin 2 Kings 14. 6.
The wages of sin is death . . . Rom. 6. 23; Jas. 1. 15.
The soul that sinneth, it shall die . . . Ezek. 18. 4, 20.

By the Law is the knowledge of sin . . Rom. 3. 20.

WHAT IS SIN?

In the multitude of words . . . Prov. 10. 19.
The thought of foolishness . . . Prov. 24. 9.
Whatsoever is not of faith . . . Rom. 14. 23.
Knowing to do good, and doing it not . . James 4. 17.
The transgression of the law . . . 1 John 3. 4.
All unrighteousness . . . . 1 John 5. 17.

Pleasures of sin only for season . . . Heb. 11. 25.

HOW IS SIN REMOVED?

The blood cleanseth from all	1 John 1. 7.
Laid on Christ	Isa. 53. 6.
Put away by Christ	Heb. 9. 26.
Christ made to be sin for us	2 Cor. 5. 21.
The Lamb of God takes away	John 1. 29.
Christ Jesus came to save sinners	1 Tim. 1. 15.
Christ died for our sins	1 Cor. 15. 3.
He bare our sins, in His own body on the tree	1 Peter 2. 24.
Without shedding of blood is no remission	Heb. 9. 22.
Christ is exalted to give forgiveness	Acts 5. 31.

THE SINS OF GOD'S PEOPLE.

As white as snow; as wool	Isa. 1. 18.
Forgiven, and covered	Ps. 85. 2.
Removed as far as the east is from the west	Ps. 103. 12.
Remembered no more	Heb. 10. 17.
Cast behind God's back	Isa. 38. 17.
Cast into the depths of the sea	Micah 7. 19.
Blotted out as a thick cloud	Isa. 44. 22.
If we confess our sins, He is faithful and just to forgive us our sins, &c.	1 John 1. 9.

VICTORY OVER SIN.

His name Jesus, for He shall save His people from their sins	Matt. 1. 21.
Redeemed from all iniquity	Titus 2. 14.
Sin no dominion over—free from	Rom. 6. 14, 22.
Whosoever abideth in Him, sinneth not	1 John 3. 6.
I thank God, through Jesus Christ	Rom. 7. 25.
Always to triumph in Christ	2 Cor. 2. 14.
This is the victory that overcometh, even our faith	1 John 5. 4.
He is able to keep you from falling	Jude 24.
I can do all things through Christ	Phil. 4. 13.

PLEASURES.
A CONTRAST.

The pleasures of sin for a season . . .	Heb. 11. 25.
She that liveth in pleasure is dead while she liveth	1 Tim. 5. 6.

Thou shalt make them drink of the river of Thy pleasures	Ps. 36. 8.
At Thy right hand there are pleasures for evermore	Ps. 16. 11.

SEVEN "GREAT" THINGS.

Great . .	Salvation . .	Heb. 2. 3.
Great . .	Love . .	Eph. 2. 4.
Great . .	Peace . .	Ps. 119. 165.
Great . .	Joy . . .	Luke 2. 10.
Great . .	Goodness . .	Ps. 31. 19.
Great . .	Mercy . .	Ps. 103. 11.
Great . .	Faithfulness . .	Lam. 3. 23.

"GREAT THINGS" OF THE LORD.

Past . . .	Deut. 10. 21; 1 Sam. 12. 24; 2 Sam. 7. 21, 23; Ps. 71. 19; 106. 21; 126. 2, 3; Luke 1. 49; 8. 39.
Present . .	Job 5. 9; 9. 10; 37. 5; Mark 3. 8 (Heb. 13. 8).
Future . .	Jer. 33. 3; Joel 2. 21; contrast Jer. 45. 5.

"THE BOOKS OPENED."
DAN. 7. 10; REV. 20. 12.

Book of the law . . .	Deut. 30. 10; 31. 26; Gal. 3. 10.
Book of remembrance . . .	Ps. 56. 8; 139. 16; Mal. 3. 16.
Book of life	Phil. 4. 3; Rev. 3. 5; 17. 8; 20. 12, 15; 21. 27.

RESULTS OF OBEDIENCE.

Protection, and healing	Exodus 23. 21-25.
Prosperity, and good success	Joshua 1. 8.
Fruitfulness, and satisfaction	Isa. 1. 19.
Fellowship with God	John 14. 21, 23; 15. 10.
Knowledge of God	1 John 2. 3-5.
Prayer answered	John 14. 14 with 15; 1 John 3. 22.
The Holy Ghost given	Acts 5. 32.
Eternal salvation	Heb. 5. 9.
We abide in Him, and He in us	1 John 3. 24.

"PEACE, PEACE."

When there is no peace	Jer. 6. 14; 8. 11.
To him that is afar off, and to him that is near	Isa. 57. 19.
Thou wilt keep him in perfect peace (margin)	Isa. 26. 3.
I leave with you—I give unto you	John 14. 27.
He is our peace . . . made peace	Eph. 2. 14; Col. 1. 20.

LIMITING CHRIST'S POWER.

JOHN 11.

As to *place*—
    If Thou hadst been *here*, my brother had not died . . . . . John 11. 21, 32.

As to *time*—
    I know that He shall rise again *in the resurrection, at the last day*. . . John 11. 24.

As to *extent*—
    By this time he *stinketh—dead four days* . John 11. 39.

The Lord's answer—
    Said I not unto thee, that if thou wouldest believe, thou shouldest see the glory of God? . . . . . John 11. 40; with Ps. 27. 13.

"I AM WITH THEE."

I am with thee, and will bless thee	Gen. 26. 24, 28.
I am with thee, and will keep thee in all places	Gen. 28. 15.
I am with thee: be not dismayed	Isa. 41. 10.
I am with thee: fear not	Isa. 43. 5.
I am with thee to deliver thee	Jer. 1. 8, 19
I am with thee to save thee	Jer. 15. 20; 30. 11.
I am with thee, to correct thee in measure	Jer. 46. 28.
I am with thee, and no man shall set on thee to hurt thee	Acts 18. 10; with Matt. 28. 20.

"I WILL BE WITH THEE."

I will be with thee (and will bless thee)	Gen. 26. 3. (Isaac).
I will be with thee (to protect)	Gen. 31. 3. (Jacob).
I will be with thee (certainly)	Exod. 3. 12. (Moses).
I will be with thee (to guide)	Deut. 31. 23. (Joshua).
I will be with thee (not fail, nor forsake)	Josh. 1. 5. (Joshua).
I will be with thee (according to promise)	Josh. 3. 7. (Joshua).
I will be with thee (to build thee a sure house)	1 Kings 11. 38. (Jeroboam).
I will be with thee (when thou passest through the waters)	Isa. 43. 2. (Jacob and Israel).

THE EYES OF THE LORD

Are in every place	Prov. 15. 3.
Run to and fro throughout the whole earth	2 Chron. 16. 9; Zech. 4. 10.
The ways of man are before	Prov. 5. 21; Jer. 16. 17; 32. 19.
Upon the haughty	2 Sam. 22. 28.
Upon the sinful kingdom	Amos 9. 8.
Set upon them for evil	Amos 9. 4.
Upon the righteous, &c.	Ps. 34. 15; 33. 18; 101. 6.
Always upon it (the land, the house)	Deut. 11. 12; 1 Kings 9. 3.
Upon them for good	Jer. 24. 6.
Upon me	Job 7. 8.
Did see my substance	Ps. 139. 16.
Preserve knowledge	Prov. 22. 12.
Are not Thine eyes upon the truth?	Jer. 5. 3.

GOD THE ROCK.

He is the Rock	Deut. 32. 4.
Jeshurun lightly esteemed the Rock of his salvation	Deut. 32. 15.
Of the Rock that begat thee, thou art unmindful	Deut. 32. 18.
Their Rock	Deut. 32. 30.
Our Rock	Deut. 32. 31.
Neither is there any Rock like our God	1 Sam. 2. 2.
The Rock of Israel spake to me	2 Sam. 23. 3.
The Lord is my Rock	Ps. 18. 2.
Who is a Rock save our God?	Ps. 18. 31.
Blessed be my Rock	Ps. 18. 46.
O Lord, my Rock (margin), and my Redeemer	Ps. 19. 14.
He shall set me up upon a Rock	Ps. 27. 5.
Unto Thee will I cry, O Lord, my Rock	Ps. 28. 1.
Be Thou my strong Rock	Ps. 31. 2.
For Thou art my Rock	Ps. 31. 3.
He set my feet upon a Rock	Ps. 40. 2.
I will say unto God my Rock	Ps. 42. 9.
Lead me to the Rock that is higher than I	Ps. 61. 2.
He only is my Rock, and my salvation	Ps. 62. 2, 6.
The Rock of my strength . . . is in God	Ps. 62. 7.
Thou art my Rock and my fortress (see margin)	Ps. 71. 3.
God is the Rock of my heart (margin)	Ps. 73. 26.
They remembered that God was their Rock	Ps. 78. 35.
Thou art . . . the Rock of my salvation	Ps. 89. 26.
He is my Rock, and there is no unrighteousness in Him	Ps. 92. 15.
My God is the Rock of my Refuge	Ps. 94. 22.
Let us make a joyful noise to the Rock of our Salvation	Ps. 95. 1.
Thou hast not been mindful of the Rock of thy strength	Isa. 17. 10.
The Lord Jehovah is the "Rock of Ages" (marg.)	Isa. 26. 4.
The Rock of Israel (margin)	Isa. 30. 29.
The shadow of a great Rock in a weary land	Isa. 32. 2.
Is there a Rock beside Me? (margin)	Isa. 44. 8.
O mighty Rock, Thou hast established them for correction (margin)	Hab. 1. 12.
That Rock was Christ	1 Cor. 10. 4.

"A LITTLE REVIVING."
Ezra 9. 8.

O Lord, *revive* Thy work	Hab. 3. 2.
Wilt Thou not *revive* us again?	Ps. 85. 6.
After two days will He *revive* us	Hosea 6. 2.
To *revive* the spirit of the humble	Isa. 57. 15.
To *revive* the heart of the contrite	Isa. 57. 15.
They shall *revive* as the corn	Hosea 14. 7.
Though I walk in the midst of trouble, Thou wilt *revive* me	Ps. 138. 7.

THREE CROWNS.
Contrast John 19. 5.

A crown of righteousness—
    Unto all them that love His appearing . 2 Tim. 4. 8.
A crown of life—
    To them that love Him . . . that endure temptation . Jas. 1. 12; Rev. 2. 10.
A crown of glory—
    To the shepherds of the flock . 1 Peter 5. 4.

    See also 1 Cor. ix. 25; Phil. iv. 1; 1 Thess. ii. 19; and Rev. iv. 4, 10.

WALK.

After God. Obedience.

Deut. 13. 4; 2 Kings 23. 3; Ps. 63. 8; Hosea 6. 3; 11. 10; Matt. 10. 38; John 21. 22; 1 Peter 2. 21.
Example—Caleb. Our eyes on Him. Numb. 14. 24; Ps. 123. 1, 2.

Before God. Sincerity.

Gen. 17. 1; 24. 40; 1 Kings 2. 4; 2 Kings 20. 3; Ps. 56. 13.
Example—Abraham. His eyes on us. Gen. 48. 15; Ps. 34. 15.

With God. Companionship.

Amos 3. 3; Micah 6. 8 (marg.); Mal. 2. 6; 2 Cor. 6. 16; Rev. 3. 4.
Example—Enoch. Gen. 5. 22, 24; Heb. 11. 5; Song of Sol. 8. 5.

WE ARE NOT ABLE; GOD IS ABLE.

"I CAN DO ALL THINGS THROUGH CHRIST."—PHIL. 4. 13.

Moses said—

    "Who am I, that I should go?" . . Exod. 3. 11.
    "What shall I say unto them?" . . Exod. 3. 13.
    "I am not eloquent . . . slow of speech" . Exod. 4. 10.

God said—

    "*I* will send thee" . . . . Exod. 3. 10.
    "Certainly *I* will be with thee . . . *I* have sent thee" . . . . Exod. 3. 12.
    "*I* am that *I* am" . . . . Exod. 3. 14.
    "*I* will be with thy mouth" . . . Exod. 4. 12, 15.

Gideon said—

    "Wherewith shall I save Israel? . . . I am the least in my Father's house . . Judges 6. 15.

God said—

    "Have not *I* sent thee?" . . . Judges 6. 14.
    "Surely *I* will be with thee" . . . Judges 6. 16.

Jeremiah said—

    "Ah, Lord God! behold, I cannot speak: for I am a child . . . . Jer. 1. 6.

God said—

    "*I* formed thee . . . *I* knew thee . . . *I* sanctified thee . . . *I* ordained thee" . Jer. 1. 5.
    "Thou shalt go . . . *I* send thee . . . whatsoever *I* command thee thou shalt speak" . . . . . Jer. 1. 7.
    "*I* am with thee to deliver thee" . . Jer. 1. 8.
    "*I* have put *My* words in thy mouth" . Jer. 1. 9.
    "*I* have this day set thee over the nations" Jer. 1. 10.
    "*I* will hasten *My* word to perform it" . Jer. 1. 12.

"STAND STILL,"

"And see the salvation of the Lord"	Exod. 14. 13.
"And I will hear what the Lord will command"	Numb. 9. 8.
"In Jordan"	Joshua 3. 8.
"That I may shew thee the word of God"	1 Sam. 9. 27.
"That I may reason with you before the Lord"	1 Sam. 12. 7.
"And see the salvation of the Lord with you"	2 Chron. 20. 17.
"And consider the wondrous works of God"	Job 37. 14.

WINGS (HIS).

He bears us on	Exod. 19. 4; Deut. 32. 11.
He heals with	Mal. 4. 2.
He gathers under	Matt. 23. 37.
We trust under	Ps. 91. 4; Ruth 2. 12; Ps. 36. 7; 61. 4.
We are hidden under	Ps. 17. 8.
We make our refuge under	Ps. 57. 1.
We rejoice under	Ps. 63. 7.

EFFECT OF AN UNGODLY AFFINITY.

2 CHRON. 18. 1–3; 20. 35, 36; 21. 6.

Jehoshaphat himself defeated in battle	2 Chron. 18. 31; 20. 37.
All his sons die unnatural deaths	2 Chron. 21. 4.
His eldest, Jehoram, "smitten of the Lord"	2 Chron. 21. 18.
All his grandsons die by violence	2 Chron. 21. 17; 22. 9.
All his great-grandsons also	2 Chron. 22. 8, 10; 24. 25.

2 Chron. 19. 2; with 2 Cor. 6. 14–18.

THE DEVIL-POSSESSED MAN.

MARK 5. 2–7, 15, 18; with LUKE 8.

No home—living among the dead—nothing to do with Jesus—no rest—unclothed—hurting himself—afraid of Christ. "Torment me not."

Afterwards. Sitting—clothed in his right mind—"prayed Him that he might be with Him"—told his friends.

INSTANCES OF EARLY RISING IN THE SERVICE OF GOD.

Abraham rose early to stand before the Lord	Gen. 19. 27.
Abraham rose early to send away Hagar	Gen. 21. 14.
Abraham rose early to sacrifice Isaac	Gen. 22. 3.
Jacob rose early to sacrifice unto the Lord	Gen. 28. 18.
Moses rose early to give God's message to Pharaoh	Exod. 8. 20.
Moses rose early to give another message to Pharaoh	Exod. 9. 13.
Moses rose early, and builded an altar to God	Exod. 24. 4.
Moses rose early to meet with God at Sinai	Exod. 34. 4.
Joshua rose early to go to Jordan, before they passed over	Joshua 3. 1.
Joshua rose early to compass the city of Jericho	Joshua 6. 12.
Joshua rose early to find out the sin of the camp	Joshua 7. 16.
Joshua rose early to go up against Ai.	Joshua 8. 10.
Gideon rose early to see what God had done to the fleece	Judges 6. 38.
Hannah and Elkanah rose early to worship God	1 Sam. 1. 19.
Samuel rose early to meet Saul about the Amalekites	1 Sam. 15. 12.
David rose early to do as his father bid him	1 Sam. 17. 20.
Israel rose early, and saw their enemies dead	2 Kings 19. 35.
Jehoshaphat rose early against the Ammonites	2 Chron. 20. 20.
Job rose early to offer burnt-offerings for his children	Job 1. 5.
Jesus rose early to go to a solitary place to pray	Mark 1. 35.
The women rose early to go to the sepulchre	Mark 16. 2.
The people rose early to go to the temple, to hear Jesus	Luke 21. 38.
Jesus rose early to go to the temple, to teach the people	John 8. 2.
The apostles rose early to teach in the temple	Acts 5. 21.

JEHOVAH.

Jehovah Jireh,	The Provider	Gen. 22. 14.
Jehovah Rophi,	The Healer	Exod. 15. 26.
Jehovah Nissi,	My Banner	Exod. 17. 15.
Jehovah Shalom,	Send Peace	Judges 6. 24.
Jehovah Sabaoth,	Of Hosts	Isa. 6. 3; Jer. 46. 18.
Jehovah Tsidkenu,	Our Righteousness	Jer. 23. 6; 33. 16.
Jehovah Gmolah,	The Recompenser	Jer. 51. 56.
Jehovah Makkeh,	The Smiter	Ezek. 7. 9.
Jehovah Mekaddesham,	The Sanctifier	Ezek. 20. 12; Exod. 31. 13.
Jehovah Shammah,	"Is there"	Ezek. 48. 35.

JEHOVAH ROPHI

(THE HEALER).

I am the Lord that healeth thee	Exod. 15. 26.
I wound, and I heal	Deut. 32, 39.
He hath torn, and He will heal us.	Hosea 6. 1.
The Lord healeth the stroke of their wound	Isa. 30. 26.
I will heal thee of thy wounds	Jer. 30. 17.
O Lord, heal me	Ps. 6. 2.
Heal my soul	Ps. 41. 4.
Heal me, and I shall be healed	Jer. 17. 14.
I cried unto Thee, and Thou hast healed me	Ps. 30. 2.
He sent His word, and healed them	Ps. 107. 20.
With His stripes we are healed	Isa. 53. 5; 1 Pet. 2. 24.
He healeth the broken in heart	Ps. 147. 3; Luke 4. 18.
Who healeth all thy diseases	Ps. 103. 3.
I have seen his ways, and will heal him	Isa. 57. 18.
They knew not that I healed them	Hosea 11. 3.
I will heal their backsliding	Hosea 14. 4.
Unto you that fear my name, shall the Sun of righteousness arise with healing in His wings	Mal. 4. 2.

JEHOVAH JIREH
(THE PROVIDER).

God *will provide* Himself a lamb.	Gen. 22. 8, 14.
I have *provided* Me a king among his sons	1 Sam. 16. 1.
Who *provideth* for the raven his food	Job 38. 41.
Can He *provide* flesh for His people?	Ps. 78. 20 with 24.
Thou preparest them corn, when Thou hast so *provided* for it	Ps. 65. 9.
God having *provided* some better thing for us	Heb. 11. 40.

See also Phil. 4. 19; therefore Rom. 13. 14.

"IN THE LORD."
Isaiah 45.

Everlasting salvation	Isa. 45. 17.
Righteousness	Isa. 45. 24.
Strength	Isa. 45. 24.
Justification	Isa. 45. 25.
Glory	Isa. 45. 25.

STEPS.

"Not in man that walketh to direct His steps"	Jer. 10. 23.
"The Lord directeth his steps"	Prov. 16. 9.
"Thou numberest my steps"	Job 14. 16.
"Doth not He count all my steps?"	Job 31. 4.
"Thou hast enlarged my steps under me"	Ps. 18. 36.
"The steps of a good man are ordered by the Lord"	Ps. 37. 23.
"None of his steps shall slide"	Ps. 37. 31.
"Order my steps in Thy word"	Ps. 119. 133.
"When thou goest thy steps shall not be straitened.	Prov. 4. 12; contrast Job 18. 7.

"HIS STEPS."

"Follow His steps"	1 Peter 2. 21.
"Shall set us in the way of His steps"	Ps. 85. 13.
"My foot hath held His steps"	Job 23. 11.

FOUR STEPS
(IN ONE DAY).

Looking upon Jesus	John 1. 36.
Following Jesus	John 1. 37.
Abiding with Jesus	John 1. 39.
Bringing others to Jesus	John 1. 42.

FOUR MORE STEPS.
LUKE 5.

Failure	"Taken nothing"	Luke 5. 5.
Faith	"Nevertheless at Thy word"	Luke 5. 5.
Fulness	"A great multitude of fishes"	Luke 5. 6.
Fellowship	"They beckoned unto partners"	Luke 5. 7.

SEE ALSO FOUR MORE.

"He left all"
"Rose up"
"Followed Him"
"Made Him a great feast," and invited others
} Luke 5. 28, 29.

LOT'S DOWNWARD AND UPWARD STEPS.
DOWNWARD.

"Beheld all the plain of Jordan"	Gen. 13. 10.
"Chose him all the plain of Jordan"	Gen. 13. 11.
"Journeyed east" (left Abraham)	Gen. 13. 11.
"Pitched his tent toward Sodom"	Gen. 13. 12.
"Dwelt in Sodom"	Gen. 14. 12.
"Sat in the gate of Sodom" (a judge, *v.* 9)	Gen. 19. 1.
Married his children to Sodomites	Gen. 19. 14.

UPWARD.

"Brought forth without the city"
"Escape for thy life"
Sodom destroyed
"God remembered Abraham, and sent Lot out"
"Lot dwelt in the mountain" (*v.* 17)
} Gen. 19. 16, 17, 24, 25, 29, 30.

See also 2 Peter 2. 6-8.

DAVID'S DOWNWARD AND UPWARD STEPS.
DOWNWARD.

"I shall now perish." What a strange sequel to chap. 26!
"He passed over unto Achish"
"And David dwelt with Achish"
"Give me a place . . . in the country"
"Achish gave him Ziklag"
"David smote the land, returned, and came to Achish"
"David said, against the south of Judah" (a lie)
Achish's "servant for ever"
"Shalt know what thy servant can do"

1 Sam. 27. 1–3, 5, 6, 9, 10, 12; 28. 2.

Notice chap. 29. 3-5. The world would not have him.

UPWARD.

"Rose up early to depart"
"Ziklag burned with fire"
"Encouraged himself in the Lord"
"Enquired at the Lord"
"David recovered all"

1 Sam. 29. 11; 30. 1, 6, 8. 18.

PETER'S DOWNWARD AND UPWARD STEPS.
DOWNWARD.

Boastful and self-confident	Matt. 26. 33, 35.
Sleepy (too lazy to watch)	Matt. 26. 40.
Forsook Jesus (gave up near communion)	Matt. 26. 56.
Followed afar off (lost sight of Jesus)	Matt. 26. 58.
Sat without (made himself one with servants)	Matt. 26. 69.
Denied (told an untruth)	Matt. 26. 70.
Denied with an oath (lost all courage)	Matt. 26. 72.
Began to curse and to swear	Matt. 26. 74.

UPWARD.
RESULTING FROM THE LORD'S LOOK (Luke 22. 61).

Peter remembered	Matt. 26. 75.
Went out (turned his back on the world)	Matt. 26. 75.
Wept bitterly (deep contrition)	Matt. 26. 75.
"Go, tell His disciples *and Peter*"	Mark 16. 7.

PRAYER AND PRAISE
(TOGETHER).

1 Chron. 16. 8, 11.	2 Chron. 20. 18, 19.
Neh. 9. 1, 5.	Neh. 11. 17.
Ps. 50. 14, 15.	Ps. 72. 15.
Phil. 4. 6.	1 Thess. 5. 17, 18.

HATH—WILL
(IN PSALMS).

The Lord hath heard.	He will receive my prayer	Ps. 6. 9.
Thou hast heard.	Thou wilt hear.	Ps. 10. 17.
Thou hast been my help.	The Lord will take me up.	Ps. 27. 9, 10.
He hath delivered.	He shall hear.	Ps. 55. 18, 17.
Thou hast holden me.	Thou shalt guide me.	Ps. 73. 23, 24.
He hath given meat.	He will ever be mindful	Ps. 111. 5.
The Lord hath been mindful.	He will bless us.	Ps. 115. 12.

EVERLASTING
(IN ISAIAH).

God	Isa. 40. 28.
Father	Isa. 9. 6.
Covenant	Isa. 55. 3.
Sign	Isa. 55. 13.
Salvation	Isa. 45. 17.
Name	Isa. 56. 5; 63. 12, 16.
Strength	Isa. 26. 4.
Kindness	Isa. 54. 8.
Joy	Isa. 35. 10; 51. 11.
Burnings	Isa. 33. 14.
Light	Isa. 60. 19, 20.

WHERE THE LORD IS.

The Lord is	Before His people		.	.	Micah 2. 13; John 10. 4.
"	Behind	"	.	.	Ps. 139. 5; Isa. 58. 8.
"	Above	"	.	.	Deut. 33. 12; Ps. 63. 7; 91. 1.
"	Beneath	"	.	.	Deut. 32. 11; 33. 27; Isa. 40. 11; 46. 4.
"	Around	"	.	.	Ps. 125. 2; 139. 3.
"	With .	"	.	.	Isa. 41. 10; Numb. 23. 21; Matt. 1. 23; 28. 20.
"	In the midst of	"	.	.	Isa. 12. 6; Zeph. 3. 17.
"Abide in Me, and I in you"			.	.	John 15. 4.

THE LORD IS EXCELLENT.

Excellent in His name	.	.	.	Ps. 8. 1, 9.
"	greatness	.	.	.	Ps. 150. 2.
"	loving-kindness	.	.	.	Ps. 36. 7.
"	power	.	.	.	Job 37. 23.
"	judgment	.	.	.	Job 37. 23.
"	plenty of justice	.	.	.	Job 37. 23.
"	working	.	.	.	Isa. 28. 29.
"He hath done excellent things"	.	.	.	Isa. 12. 5.

GOD IS OUR
(IN PSALMS).

Stay	.	.	.	.	Ps. 18. 18.
Shepherd	.	.	.	.	Ps. 23. 1.
Salvation	.	.	.	.	Ps. 27. 1.
Strength	.	.	.	.	Ps. 28. 7.
Sun	.	.	.	.	Ps. 84. 11.
Song	.	.	.	.	Ps. 118. 14.
Shield	.	.	.	.	Ps. 119. 114.
Shade	.	.	.	.	Ps. 121. 5.

THE GOD OF

My salvation	Ps. 18. 46.
,,	Ps. 25. 5.
,,	Ps. 27. 9.
,,	Micah 7. 7.
,,	Hab. 3. 18.
,,	Isa. 12. 2.
Thy salvation	Isa. 17. 10.
His salvation	Ps. 24. 5.
Our salvation	1 Chron. 16. 35.
,,	Ps. 65. 5.
,,	Ps. 68. 19.
,,	Ps. 79. 9.
,,	Ps. 85. 4.

See also 2 Sam. 22. 3, 36, 47, 51; and 2 Sam. 23. 5.

THE LORD "A LEADER"

(IN ISAIAH).

PAST.

So didst Thou lead Thy people	Isa. 63. 14.
Led them with His glorious arm	Isa. 63. 12.
Led them through the deep	Isa. 63. 13.
Led them through the deserts	Isa. 48. 21.

PRESENT.

A Leader to the people	Isa. 55. 4.
Which leadeth thee	Isa. 48. 17.

FUTURE.

I will lead him also	Isa. 57. 18.
I will lead them in paths that they have not known	Isa. 42. 16.
He that hath mercy on them shall lead them	Isa. 49. 10.
He shall gently lead	Isa. 40. 11.
Ye shall be led forth with peace	Isa. 55. 12.

THE LORD A FOUNTAIN.

With Thee is the fountain of life	Ps. 36. 9.
The fear of the Lord is a fountain of life	Prov. 14. 27.
They have forsaken the fountain of living waters	Jer. 2. 13; 17. 13.
In that day there shall be a fountain opened	Zech. 13. 1.
I will give the fountain of the water of life freely	Rev. 21. 6.
The Lamb shall lead them unto living fountains of waters	Rev. 7. 17.

SATISFACTION.
A CONTRAST.

⎧ No satisfaction for the life of a murderer, guilty of death	Numb. 35. 31; Ezek. 18. 4, 20.
⎩ He shall see of the travail of His soul, and shall be satisfied.... He shall bear their iniquities	Isa. 53. 11; 2 Cor. 5. 18, 19, 21.
⎧ They shall not satisfy their souls	Ezek. 7. 19.
⎩ He satisfieth the longing soul. My soul shall be satisfied	Ps. 107. 9; 63. 5.
⎧ From whence can a man satisfy these men with bread here in the wilderness?	Mark 8. 4.
⎩ He satisfied them with the bread of heaven	Ps. 105. 40; John 6. 48-51.
⎧ Ye shall eat, and not be satisfied	Lev. 26. 26.
⎨ The meek shall eat, and be satisfied	Ps. 22. 26.
⎩ Who satisfieth thy mouth with good	Ps. 103. 5.
⎧ Wherefore do ye spend money for that which is not bread? and your labour for that which satisfieth not?	Isa. 55. 2; Eccles. 5. 10.
⎩ My people shall be satisfied with My goodness, saith the Lord	Jer. 31. 14.
⎧ The eyes of man are never satisfied	Prov. 27. 20.
⎨ The eye is not satisfied with seeing	Eccles. 1. 8; 4. 8.
⎩ I shall be satisfied, when I awake, with Thy likeness	Ps. 17. 15.
⎧ O satisfy us early with Thy mercy; that we may rejoice, and be glad all our days	Ps. 90. 14.
⎩ They shall be abundantly satisfied with the fatness of Thy house	Ps. 36. 8; 65. 4.

See also Prov. 19. 23.

PARTAKERS

Of the gospel	1 Cor. 9. 23.
Of the afflictions of the gospel	2 Tim. 1. 8.
Of His promise in Christ by the gospel	Eph. 3. 6.
Of grace	Phil. 1. 7.
Of chastisement	Heb. 12. 8.
Of Christ's sufferings	1 Peter 4. 13.
Of the sufferings, so also of the consolation	2 Cor. 1. 7.
Of sufferings, that we may be "partakers of His holiness"	Heb. 12. 10.
Of the inheritance of the saints in light	Col. 1. 12.
Of that one bread	1 Cor. 10. 17.
Of the benefit	1 Tim. 6. 2.
Of the heavenly calling	Heb. 3. 1.
Of Christ	Heb. 3. 14.
Of the Holy Ghost	Heb. 6. 4.
Of the divine nature	2 Peter 1. 4.
Of the glory that shall be revealed	1 Peter 5. 1.
"Be not ye therefore partakers with them"	Eph. 5. 7.

"EXCEEDING."

The Lord is our "exceeding great reward"	Gen. 15. 1.
He is our "exceeding joy"	Ps. 43. 4.
He will make us "glad also with exceeding joy"	1 Peter 4. 13.
He presents us faultless with "exceeding joy"	Jude 24.
His power is "exceeding great"	Eph. 1. 19.
His grace is "exceeding rich and abundant"	Eph. 2. 7; 1 Tim. 1. 14.
His commandment is "exceeding broad"	Ps. 119. 96.
His promises are "exceeding great and precious"	2 Peter 1. 4.
He makes "exceeding glad with His countenance"	Ps. 21. 6.
He gives us an "exceeding weight of glory"	2 Cor. 4. 17.
He is able to do "exceeding abundantly"	Eph. 3. 20.

"AN ENTRANCE ... ABUNDANTLY."
2 Peter 1. 11.

" Enter in at the strait gate "	. . .	Matt. 7. 13.
„ "by Me" (the door)	. . .	John 10. 9.
„ "to the kingdom of God"	. .	John 3. 5; Acts 14. 22.
„ "to life"	. . .	Matt. 19. 17.
„ "to rest"	. . .	Heb. 4. 3, 8, 11.
„ "to the holiest"	. . .	Heb. 10. 19.
„ "to the joy of thy Lord"	. .	Matt. 25. 21.
„ "through the gates into the city"	.	Rev. 22. 14.

"LAY HOLD"

" On eternal life "	. . .	1 Tim. 6. 12, 19.
" Upon the hope set before us "	. .	Heb. 6. 18.

"*HOLD FAST*"

"And repent" .	. . .	Rev. 3. 3.
"That which is good"	. . .	1 Thess. 5. 21.
"The form of sound words"	. .	2 Tim. 1. 13.
"The confidence and the rejoicing"	.	Heb. 3. 6.
"The profession of faith"	. .	Heb. 10. 23; 4. 14.
"That which thou hast" .	. .	Rev. 3. 11.
"Till I come" .	. . .	Rev. 2. 25.

"OUT OF THE MIDST"—"IN THE MIDST."
Zeph. 3.

Out of the midst ... thy pride	. .	Zeph. 3. 11.

In the midst ... an afflicted and poor people ...
    they shall trust in the name of the Lord . Zeph. 3. 12.

The Lord thy God in the midst of thee is mighty;
    He will save, He will rejoice over thee with
    joy; He will rest in His love . . . Zeph. 3. 15.

JESUS IN THE MIDST.

On either side one, and Jesus in the midst	John 19. 18.
Jesus Himself stood in the midst . . . and said . . . Peace be unto you	Luke 24. 36; John 20. 19, 26.
In the midst of the throne . . . stood a Lamb as it had been slain	Rev. 5. 6.
Where two or three are gathered together in my name, there am I in the midst of them	Matt. 18. 20.

FOUR PRIVILEGES.

Look unto Jesus	Heb. 12. 2.
Learn of Jesus	Matt. 11. 29.
Lean upon Jesus	Song of Sol. 8. 5.
Live for Jesus	Phil. 1. 21.

"HIS LOVE."

His great love, wherewith He loved us	Eph. 2. 4.
In His love He redeemed them	Isa. 63. 9.
The Lord set His love upon you	Deut. 7. 7.
God commendeth His love toward us	Rom. 5. 8.
His love is perfected in us	1 John 4. 12.
He will rest in His love	Zeph. 3. 17.
Jesus said, I abide in His love	John 15. 10.

PROMISES TO FAITH.

"Through our Lord Jesus Christ."—Rom. 5. 1, 2.

Justification	"Being justified"	Rom. 5. 1.
Peace	"We have peace"	Rom. 5. 1.
Access	"Also we have access"	Rom. 5. 2.
Grace	"Into this grace"	Rom. 5. 2.
Joy	"And rejoice"	Rom. 5. 2.
Glory	"In hope of the glory"	Rom. 5. 2.

CHARACTERISTICS OF CHILDREN OF GOD
(EPISTLES OF JOHN).

Walking in the light	1 John 1. 7.
Confessing sins	1 John 1. 9.
Keeping His commandments, and word	1 John 2. 3, 5; 3. 24.
Loving our brother—the brethren	1 John 2. 10; 3. 14.
Not loving the world	1 John 2. 15.
Doing the will of God	1 John 2. 17.
Letting that abide in us, which we have heard	1 John 2. 24.
Doing righteousness	1 John 2. 29; 3. 7.
Not sinning	1 John 3. 6, 9; 5. 18.
Loving in deed and in truth	1 John 3. 18.
Confessing that Jesus is the Christ	1 John 4. 2, 15.
Loving one another	1 John 4. 7, 12.
Dwelling in love	1 John 4. 16.
Believing that Jesus is the Christ	1 John 5. 1, 10.
Overcoming the world	1 John 5. 4, 5.
Having the Son	1 John 5. 12.
Abiding in the doctrine of Christ	2 John 9.
Doing good	3 John 11.

CHARACTERISTICS OF THOSE, WHO ARE NOT THE CHILDREN OF GOD
(EPISTLES OF JOHN).

Walking in darkness	1 John 1. 6.
Saying we have no sin ... we have not sinned	1 John 1. 8, 10.
Not keeping His commandments	1 John 2. 4.
Hating our brother	1 John 2. 9, 11; 3. 15.
Loving the world	1 John 2. 15; 4. 5.
Denying that Jesus is the Christ	1 John 2. 22.
Denying the Father and the Son	1 John 2. 22.
Not doing righteousness	1 John 3. 10.
Sinning	1 John 3. 4, 6, 8.
Shutting up bowels of compassion	1 John 3. 17.
Not confessing that Jesus is the Christ	1 John 4. 3; 2 John 7.
Not loving	1 John 4. 8.
Fearing	1 John 4. 18.
Not believing God	1 John 5. 10.
Not having the Son	1 John 5. 12.
Lying in wickedness (the wicked one)	1 John 5. 19.
Not abiding in the doctrine of Christ	2 John 9.
Doing evil	3 John 11.

GRACE AND WORKS.
GRACE.

The Word was made flesh, and dwelt (tabernacled) among us ... *full of grace* and truth . . . . . John 1. 14, 16.

The law was given by Moses, but *grace* and truth *came by Jesus Christ* . . . John 1. 17.

Who hath *saved us, and called us* with an holy calling, *not according to our works, but according to His own purpose and grace,* which was given us *in Christ Jesus, before the world began* . . . . 2 Tim. 1. 9.

By grace are ye saved through faith, and that *not of yourselves:* it is *the gift of God: not of works,* lest any man should boast . Eph. 2. 8, 9.

But after that the kindness and love of God our Saviour toward man appeared, *not by works of righteousness which we have done, but according to His mercy He saved us* ... that being *justified by His grace,* we should be made heirs according to the hope of eternal life . . . . Titus 3. 4, 5, 7.

Therefore *by the deeds of the law* there *shall no flesh be justified* in His sight ... being *justified freely by His grace,* through the redemption that is in Christ Jesus . . Rom. 3. 20, 24.

Knowing that a man is *not justified by the works of the law, but by the faith of Jesus Christ,* even we have believed in Jesus Christ, that we might be *justified by the faith of Christ, and not by the works of the law:* for *by the works of the law shall no flesh be justified* . . . . . Gal. 2. 16

To him that worketh not, but believeth on Him that justifieth the ungodly, his faith is counted (imputed) for righteousness . Rom. 4. 5.

GRACE AND WORKS—*continued.*

GRACE.

If *by grace,* then is it *no more of works:* otherwise grace is no more grace. But if it be of works, then is it no more grace : otherwise work is no more work . . . Rom. 11. 6.

The God of all grace hath called us unto His eternal glory . . . . 1 Peter 5. 10.

WORKS.

We are His workmanship, *created in Christ Jesus unto good works,* which God hath before ordained (prepared) that we should walk in them . . . . Eph. 2. 10.

If a man purge himself from these, he shall be a vessel unto honour, sanctified, and meet for the Master's use, and *prepared unto every good work* . . . . 2 Tim. 2. 21.

A faithful saying, that they which have believed in God might be *careful to maintain good works* . . . . . Titus 3. 8.

In all things showing thyself *a pattern of good works* . . . . . Titus 2. 7.

A peculiar people, *zealous of good works* . . Titus 2. 14.

Even so *faith,* if it hath not works, *is dead,* being alone . . . . James 2. 17, 20, 26.

Seest thou how *faith wrought with his works, and by works was faith made perfect?* . James 2. 22.

Who is a wise man and endued with knowledge among you? let him *show out* of a good conversation *his works* with meekness of wisdom . . . . . James 3. 13.

I know thy works . . . . Rev. 2. 2, 9, 13, 19; 3. 1, 8, 15.

I will give unto everyone of you *according to your works* . . . . Rev. 2. 23.

God is not unrighteous to forget *your work and labour of love* . . . . Heb. 6. 10; 1 Thess. 1. 3.

GRACE AND WORKS—*continued.*
WORKS.

Work out your own salvation . . . *for it is God which worketh in* you . . . Phil. 2. 12, 13.

Study to show thyself approved unto God, *a workman that needeth not to be ashamed* . 2 Tim. 2. 15.

That the man of God may be perfect, *throughly furnished unto all good works* . . 2 Tim. 3. 17.

Every man's work shall be made manifest: for the day shall declare it . . . the fire shall try every man's work of what sort it is. If any man's work abide, he shall receive a reward. If any man's work shall be burned, he shall suffer loss : but he himself shall be saved ; yet so as by fire . . . 1 Cor. 3. 13-15.

Verily, verily, I say unto you, he that believeth on Me, *the works that I do shall he do also; and greater works than these* shall he do ; because I go unto My Father . John 14. 12.

I heard a voice from heaven, saying, Write, Blessed are the dead which die in the Lord from henceforth : Yea, saith the Spirit, that they may rest from their labours ; and *their works do follow them* . . . Rev. 14. 13.

See also 2 Cor. 9. 8.

"AT HAND."

The day of the Lord—" Howl ye ". . . Isa. 13. 6; Joel 1. 15; 2. 1.
„ „ " Hold thy peace " . . Zeph. 1. 7.
The kingdom of heaven—" Go preach " . . Matt. 10. 7.
The kingdom of God—"Take heed to yourselves" Luke 21. 31, 34.
The day—" Cast off the works of darkness," &c. Rom. 13. 12.
The Lord—" Let your moderation be known " . Phil. 4. 5.
The end of all things—" Be sober and watch " . 1 Peter 4. 7.
The time—" Blessed is he that readeth," &c. . Rev. 1. 3; 22. 10.

"EVERLASTING PUNISHMENT."

Everlasting burnings	Isa. 33. 14.
Everlasting contempt	Dan. 12. 2.
Everlasting fire	Matt. 18. 8; 25. 41.
Everlasting punishment	Matt. 25. 46.
Eternal damnation	Mark 3. 29.
Where their worm dieth not, and the fire is not quenched	Mark 9. 44, 46, 48; Isa. 66. 24.
Everlasting destruction	2 Thess. 1. 9.
The mist of darkness reserved for ever	2 Peter 2. 17.
Eternal fire	Jude 7.
Torment for ever and ever	Rev. 14. 10, 11; 20. 10.

SPIRITUALISM

(PASSAGES AGAINST).

Lev. 19. 26, 31; 20. 6, 27; Deut. 18. 9–14; 1 Sam. 28. 3, to end; 1 Chron. 10. 13, 14; 2 Kings 23. 24; 2 Chron. 33. 6, 11; Isa. 8. 19, 20; 19. 3, 4; 47. 9, 12–15; Jer. 27. 9, 10; Mal. 3. 5; Acts 13. 8–11; 1 Tim. 4. 1; Rev. 21. 8; 22. 15.

THE SHEPHERD.

My Shepherd	Zech. 13. 7.
One Shepherd	Ezek. 34. 23; 37. 24.
The good Shepherd	John 10. 11.
That great Shepherd	Heb. 13. 20.
The chief Shepherd	1 Peter 5. 4.
The Shepherd of your souls	1 Peter 2. 25.
My Shepherd	Ps. 23. 1.

His sheep—hear His voice—know His voice—know Him—follow Him	John 10. 4, 14, 27.

"WHOSOEVER"—"WHATSOEVER."

"*WHOSOEVER.*"

Whosoever hath sinned against Me, him will I blot out of my book.	Exod. 32. 33; Rev. 17. 8.
Whosoever denieth the Son, the same hath not the Father	1 John 2. 23.
Whosoever committeth sin transgresseth the law	1 John 3. 4.
Whosoever hateth his brother is a murderer	1 John 3. 15.
Whosoever transgresseth, and abideth not in the doctrine of Christ, hath not God	2 John 9.
Whosoever shall fall on this stone shall be broken	Matt. 21. 44.

God so loved the world, that He gave His only begotten Son, that whosoever believeth in Him should not perish, but have everlasting life	John 3. 16; also vv. 14, 15.
Whosoever believeth in Him shall receive remission of sins	Acts 10. 43.
Whosoever believeth that Jesus is the Christ, is born of God	1 John 5. 1.
Whosoever will, let him take the water of life freely	Rev. 22. 17.
Whosoever believeth on Him shall not be ashamed	Rom. 10. 11.
Whosoever shall call upon the name of the Lord shall be saved	Rom. 10. 13.

Whosoever shall humble himself as this little child, the same is greatest in the kingdom of heaven	Matt. 18. 4.
Whosoever shall exalt himself, shall be abased	Matt. 23. 12.
Whosoever doth not bear his cross, and come after Me, cannot be my disciple	Luke 14. 27
Whosoever shall confess Me before men, him will I confess before My Father which is in heaven	Matt. 10. 32, 33; Lu. 12. 8; 1 John 4. 15.
Whosoever shall give to drink to one of these little ones a cup of cold water only in the name of a disciple, . . . shall in no wise lose his reward.	Matt. 10. 42.

"WHOSOEVER"—"WHATSOEVER"—*continued.*

"*WHOSOEVER.*"

Whosoever will be chief among you, let him be your servant	Matt. 20. 27.
Whosoever shall do the will of my Father . . . the same is My brother, &c.	Matt. 12. 50.
Whosoever heareth these sayings of Mine, and doeth them, I will liken unto a wise man, &c.	Matt. 7. 24.
Whosoever is born of God sinneth not	1 John 5. 18.
Whosoever shall say unto this mountain, Be thou removed, and be thou cast into the sea, and shall not doubt in his heart, he shall have whatsoever he saith	Mark 11. 23.

"*WHATSOEVER.*"

Whatsoever we ask, we receive of Him, because we keep His commandments, and do those things that are pleasing in His sight	1 John 3. 22.
Whatsoever ye shall ask the Father in My name, He will give it you	John 16. 23; 14. 13.
Whatsoever ye shall ask in prayer, believing, ye shall receive	Matt. 21. 22.
If we know that He hear us, whatsoever we ask, we know that we have the petitions	1 John 5. 15.
Whatsoever is right, I will give you	Matt. 20. 4.

Whatsoever He saith unto you, do	John 2. 5; Gen. 31. 16.
Whatsoever ye do, do all to the glory of God	1 Cor. 10. 31.
Whatsoever ye do in word or deed, do all in the name of the Lord Jesus	Col. 3. 17.
Whatsoever ye do, do heartily, as to the Lord, and not unto men	Col. 3. 23; with Eccl. 9. 10.
Whatsoever ye have spoken in darkness, shall be heard in the light	Luke 12. 3.
Whatsoever is more than these, (yea and nay), cometh of evil	Matt. 5. 37.

He hath done whatsoever He hath pleased	Ps. 115. 3; 135. 6.
Whatsoever God doeth, it shall be for ever	Eccles. 3. 14.

CALLED—CALLING.

"THAT YE MAY KNOW, WHAT IS THE HOPE OF HIS CALLING."

His calling	Eph. 1. 18.
The high calling	Phil. 3. 14.
An holy calling	2 Tim. 1. 9.
The heavenly calling	Heb. 3. 1.
We are called saints	Rom. 1. 7; 1 Cor. 1. 2.
We are called to the fellowship of His Son Jesus	1 Cor. 1. 9.
,, peace	1 Cor. 7. 15.
,, the grace of Christ	Gal. 1. 6.
,, liberty	Gal. 5. 13.
,, His kingdom and glory	1 Thess. 2. 12.
,, holiness	1 Thess. 4. 7.
,, eternal life	1 Tim. 6. 12.
,, suffer for Christ's sake	1 Peter 2. 21.
,, inherit a blessing	1 Peter 3. 9.
,, His eternal glory	1 Peter 5. 10.
,, glory and virtue	2 Peter 1. 3.
,, the marriage supper of the Lamb	Rev. 19. 9.
"Ye see your calling, brethren"	1 Cor. 1. 26.

CONFIDENCE.

The Lord is our confidence	Prov. 3. 26; Ps. 65. 5.
In the fear of the Lord is strong confidence	Prov. 14. 26.
In confidence shall be your strength	Isa. 30. 15.
Access with confidence by the faith of Him	Eph. 3. 12.
We have confidence toward God	1 John 3. 21.
,, confidence in Him	1 John 5. 14.
,, confidence, when He shall appear	1 John 2. 28.

WITH THE WHOLE HEART.

PSALM 119.

Seeking	Ps. 119. 2, 10, 58, 145.
Praise	Ps. 119. 7 (Heb.); with Ps. 9. 1.
Obedience	Ps. 119. 34, 69.

CHILDREN, OR SONS OF GOD.

By adoption	Rom. 8. 15; Gal. 4. 5, 6.
By union with Christ	Heb. 2. 10.
By receiving Him	John 1. 12.
By faith in Him	Gal. 3. 26.
By being "led by the Spirit"	Rom. 8. 14.
By overcoming	Rev. 21. 7.
"If children . . . then heirs of God," &c.	Rom. 8. 17.

THE FUTURE OF CHILDREN OF GOD.

Glory	Heb. 2. 10.
To be like Him . . . to see Him as He is	1 John 3. 2.
Glorious liberty (resurrection life)	Rom. 8. 21.
To be gathered together in one	John 11. 52.

WHAT ARE THE CHILDREN OF GOD TO BE FILLED WITH?

The Spirit	Eph. 5. 18; Acts 2. 4.
Joy and peace in believing	Rom. 15. 13.
The knowledge of His will	Col. 1. 9.
The fruits of righteousness	Phil. 1. 11.
Wisdom, faith, and power	Acts 6. 3, 5, 8.
All the fulness of God	Eph. 3. 19.

"POOR AND NEEDY."
Psalm 70. 5; Isaiah 25. 4; 41. 17.

God does not forget	Ps. 9. 18.
God sets in safety	Ps. 12. 5.
God delivers	Ps. 35. 10; 72. 12.
God thinks upon	Ps. 40. 17.
God judges, and saves	Ps. 72. 4, 13.
God spares	Ps. 72. 13.
God raises up	Ps. 113. 7.
"Let the poor and needy praise Thy name"	Ps. 74. 21.

"YET A LITTLE WHILE."

Yet a little while,	and the wicked shall not be	Ps. 37. 10.
,,	and the indignation shall cease	Isa. 10. 25,
,,	and Lebanon shall be turned into a fruitful field	Isa. 29. 17.
,,	and I will shake the heavens, &c.	Hag. 2. 6.
,,	and the world seeth Me no more	John 14. 19; with 7. 33; 12. 35; 13. 33.
,,	and He that shall come will come	Heb. 10. 37.

TRUST

(IN PROVERBS).

With all thine heart	Prov. 3. 5.
Not to be in riches	Prov. 11. 28.
To be in the Lord	Prov. 22. 19.
Not to be in own heart	Prov. 28. 26.
In the Lord brings happiness	Prov. 16. 20.
,, ,, ,, prosperity	Prov. 28. 25.
,, ,, ,, safety	Prov. 29. 25.
,, ,, ,, protection	Prov. 30. 5.
"That thy trust may be in the Lord, I have made known to thee this day: even to thee" (see margin)	Prov. 22. 19.

THE EAGLE

Mounts up	Job 39. 27; Isa. 40. 31.
Builds high	Jer. 49. 16; Obad. 4.
Cares for its young	Deut. 32. 11; Ex. 19. 4.
Flies swiftly	Deut. 28. 49; Job 9. 26.
Lives long	Ps. 103. 5; with John 10. 10.

So also the child of God.

COMFORT

(IN ISAIAH).

"By whom shall I comfort thee?" . . . Isa. 51. 19.

PAST.

"Thou comfortedst me" . . . . Isa. 12. 1.
"The Lord hath comforted His people" . . Isa. 49. 13; 52. 9.

PRESENT.

"Comfort ye, comfort ye my people" . . Isa. 40. 1.
"Speak ye comfortably to Jerusalem" . . Isa. 40. 2.
"I, even I, am He that comforteth you" . . Isa. 51. 12.
"To comfort all that mourn" . . . Isa. 61. 2.

FUTURE.

"The Lord shall comfort Zion" . . . Isa. 51. 3.
"I will restore comforts unto him" . . Isa. 57. 18.
"As one whom his mother comforteth, so will I comfort you" . . . . Isa. 66. 13.

"CURSED"

(IN JEREMIAH).

The disobedient . . . . Jer. 11. 3.
The distrustful . . . . . Jer. 17. 5.
The deceitful . . . . . Jer. 48. 10.

"UNTIL"

Shiloh come . . . . . Gen. 49. 10.
The day break, and the shadows flee away . S. of Sol. 2. 17; 4. 6.
He come . . . . . Ezek. 21. 27; with 1 Cor. 11. 26.
The Lord come . . . . 1 Cor. 4. 5.
The day of Jesus Christ . . . . Phil. 1. 6.
The appearing of our Lord Jesus Christ . . 1 Tim. 6. 14.
The day dawn, and the day-star arise in your hearts . . . . . 2 Peter 1. 19.

ONLY.

John 3. 16; Matthew 17. 8; John 12. 9.

What God is in Himself.

The only Lord God	Jude 4.
The only Potentate	1 Tim. 6. 15.
The only true God	John 17. 3.
The only wise God	Jude 25.
Thou only art holy	Rev. 15. 4.
Who only hath immortality	1 Tim. 6. 16.
Of that day and hour knoweth ... My Father only	Matt. 24. 36.

His Part Towards Us.

He only is my Rock and my Salvation	Ps. 62. 1, 6.
Who only doeth wondrous things	Ps. 72. 18.
Thou, Lord, only makest me dwell in safety	Ps. 4. 8.
Who can forgive sins but God only?	Mark 2. 7; Ps. 51. 4.
The honour that cometh from God only	John 5. 44.

Our Part Towards Him.

Serve Him only	1 Sam. 7. 3.
Only fear the Lord	1 Sam. 12. 24.
Wait only upon God	Ps. 62. 5.
Make mention of Thy righteousness only	Ps. 71. 16.
By Thee only will we make mention of Thy name	Isa. 26. 13.

INCREASE.

"The increase of His government"	Isa. 9. 7.
"He must increase, but I must decrease"	John 3. 30.
"God that giveth the increase"	1 Cor. 3. 6, 7.
"More and more, you and your children"	Ps. 115. 14.
"By (Gr.) the knowledge of God"	Col. 1. 10.
"In love one toward another"	1 Thess. 3. 12; 4. 10.
"The meek shall increase joy in the Lord"	Isa. 29. 19.
"He increaseth strength"	Isa. 40. 29; Prov. 24. 5
"Lord, increase our faith"	Lu. 17. 5; 2 Cor. 10. 15
"The fruits of your righteousness"	2 Cor. 9. 10.
"Thou shalt increase my greatness"	Ps. 71. 21.
"The body is "the increase of God"	Eph. 4. 16; Col. 2. 19.

TREASURE.

Ye shall be a peculiar treasure unto Me	Exod. 19. 5.
The Lord shall open unto thee His good treasure	Deut. 28. 12.
The Lord hath chosen Israel for His peculiar treasure	Ps. 135. 4.
The fear of the Lord is His treasure	Isa. 33. 6.
They shall be Mine, in that day when I make up My special treasure (margin)	Mal. 3. 17.
Where your treasure is, there will your heart be also	Matt. 6. 21.
A good man out of the good treasure of the heart bringeth forth good things	Matt. 12. 35.
The kingdom of heaven is like unto treasure	Matt. 13. 44.
An householder bringeth forth out of his treasure things new and old	Matt. 13. 52.
Thou shalt have treasure in heaven	Matt. 19. 21.
We have this treasure in earthen vessels	2 Cor. 4. 7.

FOR THE SAKE.

The Lord's sake	Dan. 9. 17.
Thine own sake	Dan. 9. 19.
Mine own sake	Isa. 37. 35; 48. 11.
His great Name's sake	1 Sam. 12. 22.
Mine holy Name's sake	Ezek. 36. 22.
Thy word's sake	2 Sam. 7. 21.
Thy righteousness' sake	Ps. 143. 11.
Thy great mercies' sake	Neh. 9. 31.
Thy mercy and truth's sake	Ps. 115. 1.
Thy goodness' sake	Ps. 25. 7.
The Son of Man's sake	Luke 6. 22.
My sake, and the Gospel's	Mark 8. 35.
Christ's sake	1 Cor. 4. 10.
Jesus' sake	2 Cor. 4. 5, 11.
His sake	Phil. 1. 29.
His body's sake	Col. 1. 24.

HIDE.

I flee unto Thee to hide me (see margin)	Ps. 143. 9.
Hide me under the shadow of Thy wings	Ps. 17. 8.
In the shadow of His hand hath He hid me	Isa. 49. 2.
In His quiver hath He hid me	Isa. 49. 2.
He shall hide me in His pavilion	Ps. 27. 5.
In the secret of His tabernacle shall He hide me	Ps. 27. 5.
Thou shalt hide them in the secret of Thy presence	Ps. 31. 20.
Your life is hid with Christ in God	Col. 3. 3.
"Thy hidden ones"	Ps. 83. 3.

HIDING-PLACE.

Thou art my hiding-place	Ps. 32. 7; 119. 114.

SHADE.

The Lord is thy shade	Ps. 121. 5.

SHADOW.

The shadow of the Almighty	Ps. 91. 1; Isa. 25. 4; Isa. 32. 2.
The shadow of His hand	Isa. 49. 2; 51. 16.
The shadow of Thy wings	Ps. 17. 8; 36. 7; 57. 1; 63. 7.
The Lord's people trust under the shadow	Ps. 36. 7.
,, ,, make their refuge in	Ps. 57. 1.
,, ,, are hidden in	Isa. 49. 2.
,, ,, are covered in	Isa. 51. 16.
,, ,, sit down under (margin)	Song. of Sol. 2. 3.
,, ,, rejoice in	Ps. 63. 7.
,, ,, abide under	Ps. 91. 1.

THREE PROMISES.

PHIL. 4.

Peace—"through Christ Jesus"	Phil. 4. 7.
Power—"through Christ"	Phil. 4. 13.
Plenty—"by Christ Jesus"	Phil. 4. 19.

CARRY.

Carried all the days of old	Isa. 63. 9.
He shall carry the lambs in His bosom	Isa. 40. 11.
Even to hoar hairs will I carry you	Isa. 46. 4.
He hath carried our sorrows	Isa. 53. 4.
Carried in the Spirit	Rev. 17. 3; 21. 10.
If Thy presence go not, carry us not up hence	Exod. 33. 15.
We are carried on—His wings, His hand, His shoulders, His arms, His bosom	Ex. 19. 4; Deut. 33. 3, 12, 27; Isa. 40. 11.

THE ARM OF THE LORD.

A mighty arm	Ps. 89. 13.
A holy arm	Ps. 98. 1; Isa. 52. 10.
A glorious arm	Isa. 63. 12.
A strong arm	Jer. 21. 5; Luke 1. 51.
A high arm	Acts 13. 17.
A stretched-out arm	Exod. 6. 6; Deut. 5. 15.
An everlasting arm	Deut. 33. 27.
"Hast thou an arm like God?"	Job 40. 9.

HIS ARM

Brought salvation	Isa. 59. 16; 63. 5.
Redeems	Exod. 6. 6; Ps. 77. 15.
Rules	Isa. 40. 10.
Gathers	Isa. 40. 11.
Judges	Isa. 51. 5.
Strengthens	Ps. 89. 21.
Leads	Isa. 63. 12.
"By the greatness of Thine arm they shall be as still as a stone"	Exod. 15. 16.
Be Thou their arm every morning	Isa. 33. 2.
Put on strength, O arm of the Lord	Isa. 51. 9.
Set me as a seal upon Thine arm	Song of Sol. 8. 6.
"To whom is the arm of the Lord revealed?"	Isa. 53. 1.

QUIETNESS.

In quietness ... shall be your strength	Isa. 30. 15.
The effect of righteousness, quietness	Isa. 32. 17.
He leadeth beside the waters of quietness (marg:)	Ps. 23. 2.
When He giveth quietness, who then can make trouble?	Job 34. 29.
With quietness work	2 Thess. 3. 12.
Better is an handful with quietness	Eccl. 4. 6; Prov. 17. 1.

QUIET.

Whoso hearkeneth unto Me shall be quiet from fear of evil	Prov. 1. 33; contrast Judges 18. 7.
My people shall dwell in quiet resting-places	Isa. 32. 18.
Study to be quiet	1 Thess. 4. 11; Isa. 7. 4.
Lead a quiet and peaceable life	1 Tim. 2. 2.
Words of wise men are heard in quiet	Eccles. 9. 17.
A meek and quiet spirit is in the sight of God of great price	1 Peter 3. 4.

QUIETLY.

Quietly wait for the salvation of the Lord	Lam. 3. 26.

QUIETED.

I have quieted myself as a child	Ps. 131. 2.

CLOUDS.

IN ELIHU'S SPEECH. Job 36, and 37.

Refreshing	Job 36. 28; Ezek. 34. 26; Mal. 3. 10.
Mysterious	Job 36. 29; Ps. 139. 1-6; Isa. 42. 16.
Separating	Job 36. 32; Exod. 14. 19, 20; Isa. 44. 22.
Exhausted	Job 37. 11; Lam. 3. 44, 57, 58; 2 Cor. 4. 17, 18.
Bright	Job 37. 11; Matt. 17. 5; 2 Cor. 4. 6.
Directed	Job 37. 15; Ps. 104. 3; Hos. 2. 14; Heb. 12. 10.
Evenly balanced	Job 37. 16; Isa. 27. 8; James 1. 17.
Misunderstood	Job 37. 21; John 13. 7; 16, 19-25.
"Who can number the clouds in wisdom?"	Job 38. 37; see also Gen. 9. 13, 14.

COME.

Come	into the ark	Gen. 7. 1.
Come	with us	Numb. 10. 29.
Come	away	Song. of Sol. 2. 10, 13.
Come	now, and let us reason together	Isa. 1. 18.
Come	My people, enter into thy chambers	Isa. 26. 20.
Come	every one that thirsteth	Isa. 55. 1; Rev. 22. 17.
Come	and see	John 1. 39.
Come	and dine	John 21. 12.
Come	apart, and rest awhile	Mark 6. 31.
Come	out, and be separate	2 Cor. 6. 17.
Come	for all things are now ready	Luke 14. 17.
Come	and I will make you fishers of men	Mark 1. 17
Come	ye blessed of My Father	Matt. 25. 34.
Whosoever will may come		Rev. 22. 17.

"COME UNTO ME."

Incline your ear, and *come unto Me*	Isa. 55. 3.
Come unto Me, all ye that labour	Matt. 11. 28.
Suffer the little children to *come unto Me*	Mark 10. 14.
If any man thirst, let him *come unto Me*	John 7. 37.
"Him that cometh to Me, I will in no wise cast out"	John 6. 37; with Heb. 7. 25.

DOING RIGHTEOUSNESS.

All *our* righteousnesses filthy rags	Isa. 64. 6; Ezek 33. 12, 13.
Christ is made unto us righteousness	1 Cor. 1. 30; Jer. 23.6.
He that doeth righteousness is righteous	1 John 3. 7, with 10.

SOME RESULTS FROM

Separation unto God	2 Cor. 6. 14 to 7. 1.
Bearing witness for God	Phil. 2. 15, 16.
Love to the brethren, and to enemies	1 John 3. 14; Matt. 5. 44.
Persecution—chastisement	Matt. 5. 10; Heb. 12. 6-11.
To shine forth as the sun, in the kingdom	Matt. 13. 43.

"THE WAY."

I am the Way	John 14. 6.
This is the way	Isa. 30. 21.
A new and living way	Heb. 10. 20.
A perfect way	Ps. 101. 2, 6.
The narrow way	Matt. 7. 14.
The good way	Jer. 6. 16.
The right way	Ps. 107.7; 2 Pet. 2. 15.
The good and the right way	1 Sam. 12. 23.
The way of salvation—of His saints	Acts 16. 17; Prov. 2. 8.
The way of righteousness	Prov. 8. 20; 12. 28; 16. 31; 2 Peter 2. 21.
The way of life	Prov. 15. 24.
The way of the Spirit	Eccl. 11. 5; John 3. 8.
The way of truth	Ps. 119. 30; 2 Pet. 2.2.
The way of peace	Isa. 59. 8; Rom. 3. 17; Luke 1. 79.
The way of wisdom	Prov. 4. 11.
The way of understanding	Prov. 9. 6; Isa. 40. 14
The way of Thy precepts	Ps. 119. 27.
The way of holiness	Isa. 35. 8.
The broad way ... to destruction	Matt. 7. 13.
The way of sinners—of transgressors	Ps. 1.1; Pr. 4. 19; 13. 15.
The way to hell—of death	Pr. 7. 27; 14. 12; 16. 25.

CONTINUE

Following the Lord your God	1 Sam. 12. 14.
In My word	John 8. 31.
In My love	John 15. 9.
In the grace of God	Acts 13. 43.
In well-doing	Rom. 2. 7.
In His goodness	Rom. 11. 22.
In the faith	Col. 1. 23.
In prayer	Col. 4. 2; Ro. 12. 12.
In the doctrine	1 Tim. 4. 16.
In the things which thou hast learned, &c.	2 Tim. 3. 14;
In the perfect law of liberty	James 1. 25.
In the Son, and in the Father	1 John 2. 24.

WE KNOW.

(1 John.)

Him—and "know that we know Him"	1 John 2. 3, 4; 3. 6.
The Father	1 John 2. 13.
Him that is from the beginning	1 John 2. 13, 14.
God	1 John 4. 7.
The Spirit of God	1 John 4. 2.
That the Son of God is come	1 John 5. 20.
Him that is true	1 John 5. 20.
The truth	1 John 2. 21; see also 2 John 1.
All things	1 John 2. 20.
That He was manifested to take away our sins	1 John 3. 5.
That He is righteous	1 John 2. 29.
That every one that doeth righteousness is born of Him	1 John 2. 29.
That whosoever is born of God sinneth not	1 John 5. 18.
That we are of God	1 John 5. 19.
That we are of the truth	1 John 3. 19.
That we are in Him	1 John 2. 5.
That we dwell in Him	1 John 4. 13.
That He abideth (dwelleth) in us	1 John 3. 24.
The love that God hath to us	1 John 4. 16.
That we have passed from death unto life	1 John 3. 14.
That we love the children of God	1 John 5. 2.
That we have eternal life	1 John 5. 13; contrast ch. 3. 15.
That He heareth us	1 John 5. 15.
That we have the petitions we desired of Him	1 John 5. 15.
That it is the last time	1 John 2. 18.
The spirit of truth, and the spirit of error	1 John 4. 6.
That, when He shall appear, we shall be like Him; for we shall see Him as He is	1 John 3. 2.

REJOICE.

Those that seek the Lord	1 Chron. 16. 10.
Those that trust in the Lord	Ps. 5. 11; 33. 21.
The meek shall increase their joy in the Lord, and the poor among men shall rejoice	Isa. 29. 19.
In God	Ps. 63. 11.
In His name	Ps. 89. 16.
In the Holy One of Israel	Isa. 29. 19.
In the Lord	Phil. 3. 1; 4. 4.
In Christ Jesus	Phil. 3. 3.
In believing	1 Pet. 1. 8; Rom. 15. 13.
In His salvation	1 Sam. 2. 1.
Because I go unto the Father	John 14. 28.
At His word	Ps. 119. 162.
In the way of His testimonies	Ps. 119. 14.
Because God blesses	Deut. 16. 15.
In His great goodness	Neh. 9. 25.
In His highness	Isa. 13. 3.
In the portion He gives	Isa. 61. 7.
With others	Ps. 106. 5; 107. 42; Luke 15. 6, 9.
In their joy	Isa. 66. 10; Rom. 12. 15.
Sowers and reapers together	John 4. 36.
That Christ is preached	Phil. 1. 18.
Ministers in their people's prosperity	2 Cor. 7. 16; 1 Thess. 2. 19; 2 Joh 4; 3 Joh. 4.
For persecution	Matt. 5. 11, 12; Lu. 6. 22, 23.
Because partakers of Christ's sufferings	1 Peter 4. 13.
Because your names are written in heaven	Luke 10. 20.
In the shadow of His wings	Ps. 63. 7.
Because kept by the power of God	1 Peter 1. 5, 6.
In hope of the glory of God	Rom. 5. 2.
"Alway"—"evermore"	Phil. 4. 4; 1 Thess. 5. 16.

"FATHER."
(John 17. 24.)

The Father	1 John 1. 3.
A Father unto you	2 Cor. 6. 18.
My Father, and your Father	John 20. 17; Matt. 25. 34.
My Father	Jer. 3. 4, 19.
Thy Father	Deut. 32. 6; Matt. 6. 4; 6. 18.
Our Father	Matt. 6. 9.
Your Father	Matt. 6. 15.
His Father	Rev. 1. 6.
Their Father	Matt. 13. 43.
Abba, Father	Mark 14. 36; Rom. 8. 15; Gal. 4. 6.
Your heavenly Father	Matt. 6. 14, 26, 32.
Holy Father—Righteous Father	John 17. 11, 25.
The living Father	John 6. 57.
The everlasting Father	Isa. 9. 6.
The Father of our Lord Jesus Christ	1 Peter 1. 3; 2 Cor. 1. 3.
The Father of mercies	2 Cor. 1. 3.
The Father of spirits	Heb. 12. 9.
One Father of all	Eph. 4. 6.
A Father to Israel	Jer. 31. 9.
A Father of the fatherless	Ps. 68. 5.
The Father of lights	James 1. 17.

SEEKING AND FINDING.

"If thou shalt seek the Lord thy God, thou shalt find Him," &c.	Deut. 4. 29.
"If thou seek Him, He will be found of thee"	1 Chron. 28. 9.
"If ye seek Him, He will be found of you"	2 Chron. 15. 2, 4.
"Those that seek Me early shall find Me"	Prov. 8. 17.
"Ye shall seek Me, and find Me," &c.	Jer. 29. 13.
"Seek, and ye shall find"	Matt. 7. 7, 8.
"Seek ye the Lord while He may be found"	Isa. 55. 6; 65. 1

WE *ARE* TO SEEK.

The Lord our God	Deut. 4. 29.
The Lord	Amos 5. 6.
Him	Ps. 119. 2
Me	Prov. 8. 17; Am. 5. 4.
Jesus	Matt. 28. 5; Jno. 6. 24.
His strength	1 Chron. 16. 11.
His face	1 Chron. 16. 11.
His name	Ps. 83. 16.
His precepts	Ps. 119. 45.
All the commandments of the Lord	1 Chron. 28. 8.
To dwell in the house of the Lord	Ps. 27. 4.
Those things which are above	Col. 3. 1.
First the kingdom of God	Matt. 6. 33.
Righteousness	Zeph. 2. 3.
Meekness	Zeph. 2. 3.
Glory	Rom. 2. 7.
Honour	Rom. 2. 7.
Immortality	Rom. 2. 7.
Good, and not evil	Amos 5. 14.
The truth	Jer. 5. 1.
Peace	Ps. 34. 14.
Wisdom	Prov. 2. 4.
Knowledge	Prov. 15. 14.
Judgment	Isa. 1. 17.
That we may excel	1 Cor. 14. 12.
A city to come	Heb. 13. 14.

WE ARE *NOT* TO SEEK.

After our own heart, and our own eyes	Numb. 15. 39.
The peace of Ammon, or Moab	Deut. 23. 6.
Wizards	Lev. 19. 31.
Bethel	Amos 5. 5.
The peace of the ungodly	Ezra 9. 12.
The wealth of the ungodly	Ezra 9. 12.
Great things for ourselves	Jer. 45 5.
What we shall eat, or drink	Luke 12. 29.
Our own	1 Cor. 10. 24.

"HENCEFORTH"
IN THE NEW TESTAMENT.

Ye know the Father	John 14. 7.
We should not serve sin	Rom. 6. 6.
We should not live unto ourselves	2 Cor. 5. 15.
We know no man after the flesh	2 Cor. 5. 16.
Let no man trouble me	Gal. 6. 17.
Walk not as other Gentiles walk	Eph. 4. 17.
Thou shalt catch men	Luke 5. 10.
Not called servants, but friends	John 15. 15.
There is laid up a crown of righteousness	2 Tim. 4. 8.

SUCCESS IN PRAYER
COMES FROM

Delighting in the Lord	Ps. 37. 4; Job 22. 26. 27.
Not regarding iniquity in the heart	Ps. 66. 18; Isa. 59. 1, 2.
Believing—continuing instant	Matt. 21. 22; 15. 28; Rom. 12. 12.
Praying in His Name	John 14. 13; 15. 16; 16. 23.
Praying according to His will	1 John 5. 14, 15
Keeping His commandments	John 14. 14, 15; 1 John 3. 22.
Two of you agreeing	Matt. 18. 19.
Praying without ceasing—earnestly	1 Thess. 5. 17; Jas. 5. 16, 18.
Praying with the understanding	1 Cor. 14. 15.
Praying in the Spirit	Eph. 6. 18.

"ANYTHING."

"Is anything too hard for the Lord?"	Gen. 18. 14.
"Is there anything too hard for Me?"	Jer. 32. 27.
"Thou shalt not lack anything"	Deut. 8. 9; Lu. 22. 35.
"There failed not ought of any good thing"	Josh. 21. 45.
"They that seek the Lord shall not want any good thing"	Ps. 34. 10.
"If two of you shall agree touching any thing"	Matt. 18. 19.
"If ye shall ask any thing in My name"	John 14. 14.
"If we ask any thing according to His will"	1 John 5. 14.

"WHAT IS TRUTH?"
John 18. 38.

"O Lord God of truth"	Ps. 31. 5; Jer. 10. 10.
"I am the Truth"	John 14. 6; John 1. 17.
"The Spirit is truth"	1 John 5. 6; John 16. 13.
"Thy word is truth"	Jno. 17. 17; Da. 10. 21.
"Thy law is the truth"	Ps. 119. 142, 151.
"Thy counsels are truth"	Isa. 25. 1.
"The paths of the Lord are truth"	Ps. 25. 10.
"All Whose works are truth"	Dan. 4. 37.
"The truth is not in us"	1 John 1. 8; 2. 4.
"Ye shall know the truth, and the truth shall make you free"	John 8. 32.
"Lead *me* in Thy truth, and teach me"	Ps. 25. 5.

LIBERTY.
Gal. 4, 24 to end.

Christ proclaims	Luke 4. 18.
We have in Christ Jesus	Gal. 2. 4.
Where the Spirit of the Lord is	2 Cor. 3. 17.
We are called unto	Gal. 5. 13.
" to walk at	Ps. 119. 45.
" to look into	James 1. 25.
" to continue in	James 1. 25.
" to stand fast in	Gal. 5. 1.
" to enter into the holiest with (marg.)	Heb. 10. 19.
Not to allow it to be a stumbling-block	1 Cor. 8. 9; 10. 29.
Not to use it for an occasion to the flesh	Gal. 5. 13.
Not to use it for a cloke of maliciousness	1 Peter 2. 16.
We shall be judged by the law of	James 2. 12.
The perfect law of	James 1. 25.
Beware of liberty falsely promised	2 Peter 2. 19.
The glorious liberty of the children of God	Rom. 8. 21.

OUR LORD'S PETITIONS.

John 17.

That He, and His Father might be glorified	John 17. 1, 5.
"I pray for them"	John 17. 9.
"Keep them through Thine own Name"	John 17. 11.
"Keep them from the evil"	John 17. 15.
"Sanctify them through Thy truth"	John 17. 17.
"For them also which shall believe on Me"	John 17. 20.
"That they all may be one"	John 17. 21.
"That they may be with Me where I am"	John 17. 24.
"That they may behold My glory"	John 17. 24.

See also end of verse 26.

KNEELING IN PRAYER.

Let us kneel before the Lord our Maker	Ps. 95. 6.
Jesus kneeled down, and prayed	Luke 22. 41.
Solomon kneeled down upon his knees	2 Chron. 6. 13; 1 Kings 8. 54.
Elijah cast himself down upon the earth, and put his face between his knees	1 Kings 18. 42.
I fell upon my knees, and spread out my hands	Ezra 9. 5.
Daniel kneeled upon his knees three times a day, and prayed, and gave thanks	Dan. 6. 10; with 10. 10.
There came a man, kneeling down to Him	Matt. 17. 14; Mark 10. 17.
There came a leper, kneeling down to Him	Mark 1. 40.
Stephen kneeled down	Acts 7. 60.
Peter kneeled down, and prayed	Acts 9. 40.
Paul kneeled down, and prayed	Acts 20. 36; Eph. 3. 14.
We kneeled down on the shore, and prayed	Acts 21. 5.
In homage (*false*)	1 Kings 19. 18; Rom. 11. 4.
In mockery	Matt. 27. 29; Mark 15. 19.
Hereafter—"Every knee shall bow unto Me"	Isa. 45. 23; Rom. 14. 11; Phil. 2. 10.

Standing in prayer, two or three times only; also for praise.

GOD SEEKS,

BUT CANNOT FIND

One righteous person	Ps. 14. 2, 3; 53 2, 3.
Any good fruit	Isa. 5. 1, 2; Lu. 13. 6, 7.
Any earthly intercessor	Isa. 59. 16; 63. 5; Ezek. 22. 30.
The sins of His people	Jer. 50. 20; Mic. 7. 19.

TO FIND

That which is lost	Luke 15. 4; 19. 10.
Spiritual worshippers	John 4. 23, 24.
Fruit	Luke 20. 10; John 15. 8.
Consecration	2 Chron. 16. 9; 2 Cor. 6. 17, 18.

CHRISTIAN HOMES

(IN "THE ACTS").

The disciples'	(Jerusalem)	Acts 1. 13; 2. 1, 2.
Dorcas'	(Joppa)	Acts 9. 36.
Simon's	(Joppa)	Acts 9, 43.
Cornelius'	(Cæsarea)	Acts 10. 2; 11. 14, 15.
Mary's	(Jerusalem)	Acts 12. 12.
Disciples'	(Antioch)	Acts 14. 28.
Timothy's	(Lystra)	Acts 16. 1.
Lydia's	(Philippi)	Acts 16. 15, 40.
Jailer's	(Philippi)	Acts 16. 34.
Jason's	(Thessalonica)	Acts 17. 5, 7.
Justus'	(Corinth)	Acts 18. 7.
Crispus'	(Corinth)	Acts 18. 8.
Aquila's	(Ephesus, and Corinth)	Acts 18. 26, 3.
Disciples'	(Tyre)	Acts 21. 4, 6.
Philip's	(Cæsarea)	Acts 21. 8.
Disciples'	(Puteoli)	Acts 28. 13, 14.
Paul's	(Rome)	Acts 28. 30.

SINCERITY

In service	Josh. 24. 14.
In worship	1 Cor. 5. 8.
In conduct	2 Cor. 1. 12.
In testimony	2 Cor. 2. 17.
In love (to man)	2 Cor. 8. 8.
In love (to Christ)	Eph. 6. 24.
In doctrine	Titus 2. 7.

DOUBLE CALLS.
(NAME TWICE REPEATED.)

Saul, Saul	(conviction, and conversion)	Acts 9. 4.
Samuel, Samuel	(to service)	1 Sam. 3. 10.
Moses, Moses	(to reverence)	Exod. 3. 4.
Abraham, Abraham	(for deliverance)	Gen. 22. 11.
Simon, Simon	(of warning)	Luke 22. 31.
Martha, Martha	(of reproof)	Luke 10. 41.
Jerusalem, Jerusalem	(compassionate reproach)	Matt. 23. 37.
Jacob, Jacob	(for blessing)	Gen. 46. 2.

THE GOSPEL (GRACE AND GLORY).

"The gospel of the grace"	Acts 20. 24.
"The gospel of the glory" (Gr.)	2 Cor. 4. 4.

See Psalm 84. 11.

"GLORIOUS" THINGS
(IN THE EPISTLES).

Liberty	Rom. 8. 21.
Ministration	2 Cor. 3. 7, 8.
Gospel	2 Cor. 4. 4.
Church	Eph. 5. 27.
His body	Phil. 3. 21.
His power	Col. 1. 11.
His appearing	Titus 2. 13.

"THE SPIRIT OF"
(IN ROMANS).

Holiness	Rom. 1. 4.
Life	Rom. 8. 2.
God	Rom. 8. 9, 14.
Christ	Rom. 8. 9.
Adoption	Rom. 8. 15.

"*THE* CHRIST" (WITH ARTICLE IN GREEK)
(AS USED IN CORINTHIANS).

This seems to include "members", as well as "the Head."
1 Cor. 1. 6, 13, 17; 6. 15; 9. 12, 18; 10. 4, 9, 16; 11. 3; 12. 12; 15. 15, 22.

See also 2 Cor. 1. 5; 2. 12, 14; 3. 4; 4. 4; 5. 10, 14; 9. 13; 10. 1, 5, 14; 11. 2, 3; 12. 9; 13. 3.

Key to the whole 1 Cor. 12. 12.

SEVEN "WITHOUT"S.

Without Christ, and without God	Eph. 2. 12.
Without money, and without price	Isa. 55. 1.
Without strength ... Christ died for ungodly	Rom. 5. 6.
Without shedding of blood is no remission	Heb. 9. 22.
Without faith impossible to please Him	Heb. 11. 6.
Without holiness no man shall see the Lord	Heb. 12. 14.
Without Me ye can do nothing	John 15. 5.

"WITHOUT"
(IN HEBREWS).

Christ without sin, without spot	Heb. 4. 15; 9. 14. 28.
Without shedding of blood no remission	Heb. 9. 22, 18.
Hold fast without wavering	Heb. 10. 23.
Without faith impossible to please Him	Heb. 11. 6.
They without us not made perfect	Heb. 11. 40.
Without chastisement ... not sons	Heb. 12. 8.
Without holiness no man shall see the Lord	Heb. 12. 14.
He suffered, so let us go forth, without the camp	Heb. 13. 11 12, 13.

See also Heb. 7. 3, and 7.

IN CHRIST—OF CHRIST—AS CHRIST
(IN EPHESIANS).

All Spiritual blessings in	Eph. 1. 3.
Chosen in	Eph. 1. 4.
Accepted in	Eph. 1. 6.
Redemption in	Eph. 1. 7.
All things gathered together in	Eph. 1. 10.
An inheritance in	Eph. 1. 11.
Our trust in	Eph. 1. 12.
Sealed in	Eph. 1. 13.
His mighty power in	Eph. 1. 19, 20.
Raised up, and seated together in	Eph. 2. 6.
Grace, and kindness in (Gr.)	Eph. 2. 7.
Created unto good works in	Eph. 2. 10.
Made nigh in	Eph. 2. 13.
One new man in	Eph. 2. 15.
Fitly framed together in	Eph. 2. 21.
Builded together in	Eph. 2. 22.
Partakers of His promise in	Eph. 3. 6.
His eternal purpose in	Eph. 3. 11.
Boldness and access in	Eph. 3. 12.
Glory in the Church in (Gr.)	Eph. 3. 21.
Taught the truth in (Gr.)	Eph. 4. 21.
Forgiven in (Gr.)	Eph. 4. 32.
The God, and Father of	Eph. 1. 3, 17; 3. 14.
The blood of	Eph. 2. 13.
The prisoner of	Eph. 3. 1.
The mystery of	Eph. 3. 4.
The riches of	Eph. 3. 8.
The love of	Eph. 3. 19.
The gift of	Eph. 4. 7.
The body of	Eph. 4. 12.
The fulness of	Eph. 4. 13.
The kingdom of	Eph. 5. 5.
Servants of	Eph. 6. 6.
Walk in love as	Eph. 5. 2.
The husband is the head of the wife as	Eph. 5. 23.
,, is to love his wife as	Eph. 5. 25, 29.

"THE WHOLE ARMOUR OF GOD."

"Ye are complete in Him."—Col. 2. 10.

Light	Rom. 13. 12; John 8. 12.
Truth	Eph. 6. 14; John 14. 6.
Righteousness	Eph. 6. 14; 1 Cor. 1. 30.
Peace	Eph. 6. 15; Isa. 9. 6.
Faith	Eph. 6. 16; Heb. 12. 2.
Salvation	Eph. 6. 17; Acts 4. 12.
The Word of God	Eph. 6. 17; John 1. 1; Rev 19. 13.

See also Romans 13. 14; and 2 Cor. 6. 7.

WATCH

With Me	Matt. 26. 38, 40.
For the Master	Mark 13. 35, 37.
And pray	Matt. 26. 41.
With all perseverance	Eph. 6. 18.
For souls	Heb. 13. 17.
Daily at His gates	Prov. 8. 34.
To see what He will say	Habak. 2. 1.
Blessed is he that watcheth	Rev. 16. 15, with 3. 3.

YE ARE NOT COME UNTO   BUT YE ARE COME UNTO

Contrast Heb. 12. 18, 19 with Heb. 12. 22-24.

The mount that might be touched	Mount Sion	Ps. 2. 6; Rev. 14. 1.
That burned with fire	An innumerable company of angels	Matt. 28. 2, 3; Heb. 1. 14.
Blackness	The general assembly	Rev. 14. 1-4; 7. 9-14.
Darkness	God the judge of all	James 1. 17; 1 John 1. 5.
Tempest	The spirits of just men	Rev. 14. 5, 13.
The sound of a trumpet	Jesus the Mediator	John 1. 1; Rev. 1. 10, 15.
The voice of words	The blood that speaketh	1 Peter 1. 2.

WHY AM I A CHRISTIAN?

1. *Because* "Christ Jesus came into the world to save sinners" . . . . 1 Tim. 1. 15.
2. *Because* "the Son of God loved me, and gave Himself for me" . . . Gal. 2. 20.
3. *Because* "the blood of Jesus Christ His Son cleanseth us from all sin" . . . 1 John 1. 7.
4. *Because* "God hath given to us eternal life, and this life is in His Son". . . 1 John 5. 11.
5. *Because* "he that believeth on the Son hath everlasting life" . . . . John 3. 36.
6. *Because* "God hath also given unto us His Holy Spirit" . . . . 1 Thess. 4. 8.
7. *Because* "there is therefore now no condemnation to them which are in Christ Jesus". Rom. 8. 1.
8. *Because* "I count all things but loss, for the excellency of the knowledge of Christ Jesus my Lord" . . . . Phil. 3. 8.
9. *Because* "we know that all things work together for good to them that love God" Rom. 8. 28.
10. *Because* "I can do all things through Christ which strengtheneth me" . . . Phil. 4. 13.
11. *Because* "He hath said, I will never leave thee, nor forsake thee" . . . Heb. 13. 5.
12. *Because* "the Lord shall deliver me from every evil work, and will preserve me unto His heavenly kingdom: TO WHOM BE GLORY FOR EVER AND EVER. AMEN." 2 Tim. 4. 18.

ENQUIRY-ROOM TEXTS.

Heb. 9. 22.	1 Peter 2. 24.	John 19. 30.
Isa. 53. 6; 55. 1, 7.	2 Cor. 5. 21; 6. 2.	Rom. 6. 23; 8. 1.
Isa. 1. 18; 44. 22.	John 6. 29, 37; 7. 37.	Rev. 22. 17. [12.
Isa. 12. 2.	1 John 1. 7, to end.	Heb. 10. 17; Ps. 103.
Luke 5. 32.	Luke 19. 10.	Rom. 5. 1, 2, 8-10.
John 3. 16, 18, 36.	John 5. 24; 6. 47.	1 John 5. 10-13.
Matt. 11. 28.	John 10. 28.	1 John 2. 12.
Acts 16. 31.	Gal. 2. 20; 3. 13.	Heb. 7. 25; 13. 5.
Rom. 3. 22-26.	Rom. 10. 13.	Jude 24, 25.

SAFE—SAFETY—SAFELY.
SAFE.

Hold Thou me up, and I shall be *safe*	Ps. 119. 117.
The Name of the Lord a strong tower; the righteous runneth into it, and is *safe*	Prov. 18. 10.
Whoso putteth his trust in the Lord shall be *safe*	Prov. 29. 25.

SAFETY.

Safety is of the Lord	Prov. 21. 31.
Thou, Lord, only makest me dwell in *safety*	Ps. 4. 8.
The beloved of the Lord shall dwell in *safety* by Him	Deut. 33. 12.

SAFELY.

Whoso hearkeneth unto Me shall dwell *safely*	Prov. 1. 33.
Then shalt thou walk in thy way *safely*	Prov. 3. 23.
He led them on *safely*, so that they feared not	Ps. 78. 53.

WEIGHTS.
WHAT WE ARE TO DO WITH THEM.

Lay aside every weight	Heb. 12. 1.
Casting all your care upon Him	1 Peter 5. 7.
Cast thy burden upon the Lord	Ps. 55. 22.
Casting away his garment, he came to Jesus	Mark 10. 50; with John 11. 44.
Left their nets, and followed Him	Matt. 4. 20.
They forsook all	Luke 5. 11.
He left all, rose up, and followed Him	Luke 5. 28.
Forgetting those things which are behind	Phil. 3. 13.
No man that warreth entangleth himself	2 Tim. 2. 4.
Put off the old man	Col. 3. 9.
Cast off the works of darkness	Rom. 13. 12.
If a man purge himself from these	2 Tim. 2. 21.
If thy right eye offend thee, pluck it out, and cast it from thee. . . . . If thy right hand offend thee, cut it off, and cast it from thee	Matt. 5. 29, 30.
David girded his sword upon his armour . . and David put them off him	1 Sam. 17. 39.

FOLLOWING THE LORD.

CONSEQUENT UPON—
- Being called — Mark 1. 17, 18, 20; Luke 5. 27, 28.
- Being redeemed — Rev. 14. 4.
- Love — John 21. 15-22.
- Conviction — 1 Kings 18. 21, 39; Acts 2. 37, 41, 42.
- Being His sheep — John 10. 27.
- Being His servants — John 12. 26.
- Being His children — Eph. 5. 1.

WHOM TO FOLLOW—
- The Lord Jesus — John 1. 37; 21. 22.

WHEN TO FOLLOW—
- Immediately — Matt. 4. 22.

WHERE TO FOLLOW—
- His steps — 1 Peter 2. 21.

HOW TO FOLLOW—
- Wholly, with all the heart — Numb. 32. 11, 12; 1 Kings 14. 8.
- Leaving all, rising up — Luke 5. 28.
- Denying self, taking up cross daily — Luke 9. 23.
- Letting the dead bury their dead — Luke 9. 60.
- Hard after — Ps. 63. 8.
- As dear children — Eph. 5. 1.
- Afraid, but still following — Mark 10. 32.

RESULTS FROM FOLLOWING—
- Shall not walk in darkness — John 8. 12.
- His right hand upholdeth — Ps. 63. 8.
- To know the Lord — Hosea 6. 3.
- "Showers of blessing" — Hosea 6. 3.
- Made fishers of men — Matt. 4. 19.
- To be seen following, by the Lord — John 1. 38.
- ,, ,, by others — John 21. 20.

IN HEAVEN they follow — Rev. 14. 4; 19. 14.

"Continue following the Lord your God" — 1 Sam. 12. 14; with Hosea 6. 3.

"LITTLE CHILDREN."
1 John.

Sin not	1 John 2. 1.
Your sins are forgiven	1 John 2. 12.
Ye have known the Father	1 John 2. 13.
It is the last time	1 John 2. 18.
Abide in Him	1 John 2. 28.
Let no man deceive you	1 John 3. 7.
Love not in word, but in deed and in truth	1 John 3. 18.
Ye are of God, and have overcome	1 John 4. 4.
Keep yourselves from idols	1 John 5. 21.

THE GOSPEL.

GOOD TIDINGS . . Luke 2. 10; 8. 1; Acts 13. 32; Prov. 25.25.

ONLY BELIEVE . . Acts 16. 31; Mark 5. 36; Rom. 3. 22.

SALVATION . . . Acts 4. 12; Rom. 1. 16; Titus 2. 11.

PARDON . . . Isa. 55 7; Ps. 103. 3; Eph. 1. 7; Col. 1.14.

EVERLASTING LIFE . John 3. 16, 36; 5 24; 6. 47; Rom. 6. 23.

LIBERTY . . . Luke 4. 18; John 8. 36; Gal. 5. 1; Rom. 8. 21.

GIVING (EXAMPLES OF).

The Churches in Macedonia gave their own selves	2 Cor. 8. 5.
Hannah gave her child	1 Sam. 1. 11.
Jacob gave the tenth of all	Gen. 28. 22.
Zacchæus gave the half of his goods	Luke 19. 8.
The poor widow gave all that she had	Mark 12. 44.
"What shall *I* render unto the Lord?"	Ps. 116. 12; with Rom. 12. 1 2.

THE WORLD.

Love not the world, neither the things that are in the world	1 John 2. 15.
If any man love the world, the love of the Father is not in him	1 John 2. 15.
The world passeth away, and the lust thereof	1 John 2. 17.
The wisdom of this world is foolishness with God	1 Cor. 3 19.
The friendship of the world is enmity with God	James 4. 4.
The whole world lieth in the wicked one (Gr.)	1 John 5. 19.
What shall it profit a man, if he shall gain the whole world, and lose his own soul?	Mark 8. 36.
Demas hath forsaken me, having loved this present world	2 Tim. 4. 10.
They are of the world, therefore speak they of the world	1 John 4. 5.
Ye are of this world; I am not of this world	John 8. 23.
The cares of this world choke the word	Matt. 13. 22.
Be not conformed to this world, but be ye transformed	Rom. 12. 2.
Use this world, as not abusing it	1 Cor. 7. 31.
He that hateth his life in this world, shall keep it unto life eternal	John 12. 25.
Marvel not, if the world hate you	1 John 3. 13.
If the world hate you, ye know that it hated Me before you	John 15. 18.
If ye were of the world, the world would love his own	John 15. 19.
The world knoweth us not, because it knew Him not	1 John 3. 1.
As He is, so are we in this world	1 John 4. 17.
Greater is He that is in you, than he that is in the world	1 John 4. 4.
Be of good cheer: I have overcome the world	John 16. 33.
Whatsoever is born of God overcometh the world	1 John 5. 4.
This is the victory that overcometh the world, our faith	1 John 5. 4.

THE WORLD—*continued.*
JOHN 17.

We are given to Christ out of the world	John 17. 6.
„ left in the world	John 17. 11, 15.
„ not of the world	John 17. 14.
„ hated by the world	John 17. 14.
„ kept from the evil of the world	John 17. 15.
„ sent into the world	John 17. 18.
„ preaching the word to the world	John 17. 20, 21.
Pure religion and undefiled is this . . . to keep himself unspotted from the world	James 1. 27.
The world is crucified unto me, and I unto the world	Gal. 6. 14.
Ye are the light of the world	Matt. 5. 14.
Go ye into all the world, and preach the gospel	Mark 16. 15.

GOD'S UNANSWERED QUESTIONS.

What will ye do in the day of visitation? to whom will ye flee for help? and where will ye leave your glory?	Isa. 10. 3.
What will ye do in the end thereof?	Jer. 5. 31.
How wilt thou do in the swelling of Jordan?	Jer. 12. 5.
Who can heal thee?	Lam. 2. 13.
Can thine heart endure, or thine hands be strong, in the days that I shall deal with thee?	Ezek. 22. 14.
Where is any other that may save thee?	Hosea 13. 10.
What shall a man give in exchange for his soul?	Mark 8. 37
Shall He find faith on the earth?	Luke 18. 8.
If they do these things in a green tree, what shall be done in the dry?	Luke 23. 31.
What shall the end be of them that obey not the gospel of God?	1 Peter 4. 17.
If the righteous scarcely be saved, where shall the ungodly and the sinner appear?	1 Peter 4. 18.
How shall we escape, if we neglect so great salvation?	Heb. 2. 3.

PROMISES (UNCONDITIONAL).

God promises, *never* to—

Break His covenant	Judges 2. 1; Isa. 55. 3.
Suffer the righteous to be moved	Ps. 55. 22.
Leave us, nor forsake us	Heb. 13. 5.
Let the righteous be removed	Prov. 10. 30.
Let His people be ashamed	Joel 2. 26, 27.
Let David want a man to sit on his throne	Jer. 33. 17.
"My sheep shall never perish"	John 10. 28.

PROMISES (CONDITIONAL).

If any man love God, the same is known of Him	1 Cor. 8. 3.
If any man will do His will, he shall know of the doctrine	John 7. 17.
If ye continue in My word, then are ye My disciples indeed	John 8. 31.
If a man keep My saying, he shall never taste of death	John 8. 51, 52.
If any man serve Me, him will My Father honour	John 12. 26.
If ye forgive men their trespasses, your heavenly Father will also forgive you	Matt. 6. 14.
If any man enter in, he shall be saved, &c.	John 10. 9.
If ye abide in Me ... ye shall ask what ye will, and it shall be done unto you	John 15. 7.
If ye keep My commandments, ye shall abide in My love	John 15. 10.

NOW.

Come now	Isa. 1. 18; Luke 14. 17.
Now is the accepted time	2 Cor. 6. 2.
We have now received the atonement	Rom. 5. 11.
Now being made free from sin	Rom. 6. 22.
Now ye are clean through the Word	John 15. 3; with Ps. 119. 9.
Now are we the sons of God	1 John 3. 2.
Now is our salvation nearer	Rom. 13. 11.

THE WILL OF GOD.

Christ said—

Lo, I come to do Thy will, O God	Heb. 10. 7.
I delight to do Thy will, O my God	Ps. 40. 8.
My meat is to do the will of Him that sent Me	John 4. 34.
I seek the will of the Father	John 5. 30.
I came down, not to do Mine own will	John 6. 38.
Not as I will, but as Thou wilt	Matt. 26. 39.
Thy will be done	Matt. 26. 42.

Thy will be done in earth, as in heaven	Matt. 6. 10.
Teach me to do Thy will	Ps. 143. 10.
Filled with the knowledge of His will	Col. 1. 9.
Understanding what the will of the Lord is	Eph. 5. 17.
Live, . . . to the will of God	1 Peter 4. 2.
Stand complete in all the will of God	Col. 4. 12.
Perfect in every good work to do His will	Heb. 13. 21.
Doing the will of God from the heart	Eph. 6. 6.

PROMISES CONNECTED WITH

If any man will do His will, he shall know of the doctrine	John 7. 17.
He that doeth the will of God abideth for ever	1 John 2. 17.
He that doeth the will of My Father . . . shall enter into the kingdom	Matt. 7. 21.
He that doeth the will of My Father . . . the same is My brother, and sister, and mother	Matt. 12. 50.
If we ask anything according to His will, He heareth us	1 John 5. 14.
This is the Father's will . . . that of all which He hath given Me I should lose nothing . . . that every one which seeth the Son, and believeth on Him, may have everlasting life: and I will raise him up at the last day	John 6. 39, 40.
Having predestinated us to Himself, according to the good pleasure of His will	Eph. 1. 5.

THE WILL OF GOD—*continued*.

Of His own will begat He us with the word of truth . . . . . James 1. 18.
Having made known unto us the mystery of His will . . . . . Eph. 1. 9.
Gifts of the Holy Ghost, according to His own will . . . . . Heb. 2. 4.
I beseech you therefore . . . that ye present your bodies a living sacrifice. . . . be not conformed to this world: but be ye transformed . . . that ye may prove what is that good, and acceptable, and perfect will of God . Rom. 12. 1, 2.

"EVEN AS."

Be ye perfect, even as your Father . . is perfect Matt. 5. 48.
Forgiving one another, even as God for Christ's sake hath forgiven you . . . Eph. 4. 32; Col 3. 13.
Husbands, love your wives, even as Christ also loved the Church . . . . Eph. 5. 25.
Walk, even as He walked . . . 1 John 2. 6.
Purifieth himself, even as He is pure . . 1 John 3. 3.
Righteous, even as He is righteous . . 1 John 3. 7.
They are not of the world, even as I am not of the world . . . . . John 17. 14, 16; see also v. 22.

DIVINE DIRECTION.

It is not in man that walketh to direct his steps Jer. 10. 23.
The Lord directeth his steps . . . Prov. 16. 9.
O that my ways were directed to keep thy statutes Ps. 119. 5.
He shall direct thy paths . . . Prov. 3. 6.
The righteousness of the perfect shall direct his way . . . . . Prov. 11. 5.
I will direct their work in truth . . Isa. 61. 8.
God Himself . . . direct our way unto you . 1 Thess. 3. 11
The Lord direct your hearts into the love of God 2 Thess. 3. 5.

BE.—BE NOT.

Be ye followers of God	Eph. 5. 1.
Be filled with the Spirit	Eph. 5. 18.
Be ye doers of the Word	James 1. 22.
Be careful for nothing	Phil. 4. 6.
Be sober, be vigilant	1 Peter 5. 8.
Be ye holy, for I am holy	1 Peter 1. 16.
Be ye therefore ready also	Luke 12. 40.
Be of good cheer	John 16. 33.
Be kindly affectioned one to another	Rom. 12. 10.
Be of the same mind one toward another	Rom. 12. 16.
Be subject unto the higher powers	Rom. 13. 1.
Be ye stedfast, unmoveable, always abounding in the work of the Lord	1 Cor. 15. 58.
Be perfect, be of good comfort, be of one mind	2 Cor. 13. 11.
Be renewed in the spirit of your mind	Eph. 4. 23.
Be at peace among yourselves	1 Thess. 5. 13.
Be thou an example of the believers	1 Tim. 4. 12.
Be strong in the grace that is in Christ Jesus	2 Tim. 2. 1.
Be gentle unto all men	2 Tim. 2. 24.
Be instant in season, out of season	2 Tim. 4. 2.
Be ye also patient	James 5. 7.
Be diligent	2 Peter 3. 14.
Be watchful	Rev. 3. 2.
Be thou faithful unto death	Rev. 2. 10.
Be not afraid of them that kill the body	Luke 12. 4.
Be not conformed to this world	Rom. 12. 2.
Be not wise in your own conceits	Rom. 12. 16.
Be not overcome of evil	Rom. 12. 21.
Be ye not unequally yoked together with unbelievers	2 Cor. 6. 14.
Be not deceived; God is not mocked	Gal. 6. 7.
Be not weary in well doing	2 Thess. 3. 13; Gal. 6. 9.
Be not forgetful to entertain strangers	Heb. 13. 2.
Be not carried about with divers and strange doctrines	Heb. 13. 9.

GIFTS OF THE NEW COVENANT.

HOLINESS—
 I will put My law in their inward parts, and write it in their hearts . . . Jer. 31. 33; Heb. 8. 10.

COMMUNION—
 I will be their God, and they shall be My people . . . . . Jer. 31. 33; Heb. 8. 10.

KNOWLEDGE—
 They shall all know Me, from the least of them unto the greatest of them . . Jer. 31. 34; Heb 8. 11.

PARDON—
 I will forgive their iniquity, and I will remember their sin no more . . Jer. 31. 34; Heb. 8. 12.

"THE MASTER."

The Master saith, My time is at hand	Matt. 26. 18.
The Master is come, and calleth for thee	John 11. 28.
Mary saith unto Him, Master	John 20. 16.
Master, it is good for us to be here	Mark 9. 5.
Master, I have brought unto Thee my son	Mark 9. 17.
Master, I will follow Thee	Matt. 8. 19.
Good Master, what shall I do that I may inherit eternal life?	Mark 10. 17.
One is your Master, even Christ	Matt. 23. 8, 10.
Master, do for us whatsoever we shall desire	Mark 10. 35.
Master, Master, and kissed Him	Mark 14. 45; **see also** Luke 7. 40.
Master, Master, we perish	Luke 8. 24.
Master, we know that Thou art true	Mark 12. 14.
Master, Thou hast said the truth	Mark 12. 32.
The disciple is not above his Master	Luke 6. 40.
Ye call Me Master and Lord	John 13. 13.
If I then, your Lord and Master, have washed your feet	John 13. 14.
When once the Master of the house is risen up	Luke 13. 25.
Ye know not when the Master of the house cometh	Mark 13. 35.
A vessel . . . meet for the Master's use	2 Tim. 2. 21.

THE DEITY OF CHRIST.

He that hath seen Me, hath seen the Father, &c.	John 14. 9-11.
The Mighty God, the Everlasting Father	Isa. 9. 6.
Christ, Who is over all, God blessed for ever	Rom. 9. 5.
Emmanuel, God with us	Matt. 1. 23.
Church of God, purchased with His own blood	Acts 20. 28.
I and My Father are one	John 10. 30; 5. 17, 18.
Creator, and preserver of all things	John 1.3; Col.1.16,17; Rev. 4. 11.
Possessing the fulness of the Godhead	Col. 2. 9.
Christ is Eternal	John 8. 58; Heb. 1. 8, 10.
,, Omnipotent	Phil. 3. 21; Rev. 1. 8.
,, Omnipresent	Matt. 28. 20; John 3. 13.
,, Omniscient	John 16. 30.
,, Unchangeable	Heb. 13. 8.
Christ knows the thoughts	Luke 5. 22; with 1 Kings 8. 39.
,, forgives sins	Mark 2. 7, 10.
The Word was God, &c.	John 1. 1-3.

GIFTS OF GOD

(IN JOHN).

Power (the right) to become His sons	John 1. 12.
His only-begotten Son	John 3. 16.
Living water	John 4. 10.
The bread of life	John 6. 27, 32, 51.
The good Shepherd giveth His life for the sheep	John 10, 11.
Eternal life	John 10. 28; 17. 2.
An example	John 13. 15.
Another Comforter	John 14. 16.
Peace, My peace	John 14, 27.
Whatsoever ye shall ask the Father in My name	John 15. 16; 16. 23.
Thy word	John 17. 14, 8.
My glory	John 17. 22, 24.

CHILDREN (THOUGHTS ABOUT).

Even a child is known by his doings, whether his work be pure, and whether it be right	Prov. 20. 11.
Train up a child in the way he should go; and when he is old he will not depart from it	Prov. 22. 6.
Foolishness is bound in the heart of a child, &c.	Prov. 22. 15.
He that begetteth a wise child shall have joy of him	Prov. 23. 24; 10. 1.
Correct thy son, and he shall give thee rest	Prov. 29. 17, with 15.
Her children arise up, and call her blessed	Prov. 31. 28.
I will be a God unto thee, and to thy seed after thee	Gen. 17. 7
I know him, that he will command his children after him, and they shall keep the way of the Lord	Gen. 18. 19.
The children, which God hath graciously given thy servant	Gen. 33. 5.
Whom shall he teach knowledge?... them that are weaned from the milk, and drawn from the breasts	Isa. 28. 9.
He shall gather the lambs with His arm, &c.	Isa. 40. 11.
They brought unto Him infants, that He would touch them, &c.	Luke 18. 15, 16.
Master, I have brought unto Thee my son	Mark 9. 17.
Children are an heritage of the Lord, &c.	Ps. 127. 3.
Thy children like olive-plants round about thy table	Ps. 128. 3.
That our sons may be as plants grown up in their youth; that our daughters may be as corner stones, polished, &c.	Ps. 144. 12.
Young men and maidens; old men and children; let them praise the name of the Lord	Ps. 148. 12. 13.

CHILDREN (THOUGHTS ABOUT)
(*continued*).

The Lord shall increase you more and more, you and your children	Ps. 115. 14.
The seed of the righteous shall be delivered	Prov. 11. 21.
A just man's children are blessed after him	Prov. 20. 7.
The generation of the upright shall be blessed.	Ps. 112. 2.
The children of Thy servants shall continue, and their seed shall be established before Thee	Ps. 102. 28.
The mercy of the Lord is from everlasting to everlasting, and His righteousness unto children's children	Ps. 103. 17.
He shall save the children of the needy	Ps. 72. 4.
A Father of the fatherless	Ps. 68. 5.
Leave thy fatherless children, I will preserve them alive	Jer. 49. 11.
When my father and my mother forsake me, then the Lord will take me up	Ps. 27. 10.
Like as a father pitieth his children, so the Lord pitieth them that fear Him	Ps. 103. 13.
Hear, ye children, the instruction of a father	Prov. 4. 1.
Fathers, provoke not your children to wrath, but bring them up in the nurture and admonition of the Lord	Eph. 6. 4; with Col. 3. 21.
Children's children are the crown of old men; and the glory of children are their fathers	Prov. 17. 6.
Out of the mouth of babes and sucklings hast thou ordained strength	Ps. 8. 2.
I will pour My Spirit upon thy seed, and My blessing upon thine offspring	Isa. 44. 3.
I will save thy children	Isa. 49. 25.
All thy children shall be taught of the Lord; and great shall be the peace of thy children	Isa. 54. 13.

REDEMPTION.

None of them can by any means redeem his brother, nor give to God a ransom for him; for the redemption of their soul is precious, and it ceaseth for ever	Ps. 49. 7, 8; compare with Heb. 9. 26; and 10. 10, 18.
I the Lord am thy Saviour and thy Redeemer	Isa. 49. 26; 60. 16.
With the Lord there is *plenteous* redemption	Ps. 130. 7.
Christ hath obtained *eternal* redemption for us	Heb. 9. 12, and 15.
He hath visited and redeemed His people	Luke 1. 68; with Ps. 111. 9.
Christ is made unto us ... redemption	1 Cor. 1. 30.
Christ came to redeem them that were under the law	Gal. 4. 5.
We are justified *freely* by His grace, through the redemption that is in Christ Jesus	Rom. 3. 24; compare Isa. 52. 3.
In Whom we have redemption through His blood	Eph. 1. 7; Col. 1. 14.
Christ hath redeemed us from the curse of the law	Gal. 3. 13.
,, ,, ,, from all iniquity	Titus 2. 14; with Ps. 130 8.
,, ,, ,, our life from destruction	Ps. 103. 4; with Lam. 3. 58.
,, ,, ,, our soul from the power of the grave	Ps. 49. 15; Hos. 13. 14; Ps. 34. 22.
We are redeemed from all evil	Gen. 48. 16.
,, ,, ,, the house of bondage	Deut. 13. 5.
,, ,, ,, deceit and violence	Ps. 72. 14.
,, ,, ,, the hand of the enemy	Ps. 106. 10; with Micah 4. 10.
,, ,, ,, one stronger than we are	Jer. 31. 11; with 50. 34.
,, ,, ,, the earth	Rev. 14. 3.
,, ,, ,, among men	Rev. 14. 4.
We are redeemed with His arm	Ps. 77. 15; Ex. 6. 6.
,, ,, ,, His life	Matt. 20. 28; Mar. 10. 45.
,, ,, ,, a price	1 Cor. 6. 20; 7. 23.
,, ,, ,, His precious blood	1 Pet. 1. 19; with Rev. 5. 9.
,, ,, unto Himself a peculiar people	Titus 2. 14.
,, ,, to God	Rev. 5. 9.
O give thanks unto the Lord ... Let the redeemed of the Lord say so	Ps. 107. 1, 2; with 71. 23.

REDEMPTION—*continued.*
FUTURE.

Waiting for the redemption of our body	Rom 8. 23.
Until the redemption of the purchased possession	Eph. 1. 14.
Ye are sealed unto the Day of redemption	Eph. 4. 30.
Look up; for your redemption draweth nigh	Luke 21. 28.

See also Isa. 35. 9; and 51. 11.

Redeem us for Thy mercies' sake	Ps. 44. 26.
Is My hand shortened at all, that it cannot redeem?	Isa. 50. 2.
Fear not: for I have redeemed thee	Isa. 43. 1.
Return unto Me, for I have redeemed thee	Isa. 44. 22.
Thou hast redeemed me, O Lord God of truth	Ps. 31. 5.
O Lord, my strength, and my Redeemer	Ps. 19. 14.
I know that my Redeemer liveth	Job 19. 25.

Old Testament passages illustrating this subject: Exodus 6. 6; 13. 13-15 (with Deut. 7, 8); Lev. 25. 23 to end; also Lev. 27; Num. 3. 44 to end; Ruth 4. 1-13; Jer. 32. 6-15.

HE AND ME.

He hath done to me great things	Luke 1. 49.
He hath clothed me	Isa. 61. 10.
He hath covered me	Isa. 61. 10.
He took me	Ps. 18. 16.
He drew me	Ps. 18. 16.
He hath delivered me	Ps. 54. 7; 18. 19.
He brought me forth into a large place	Ps. 18. 19.
He delighted in me	Ps. 18. 19.
He recompensed me	Ps. 18. 20.
He hath dealt bountifully with me	Ps. 13. 6.
He hath shewed me His marvellous kindness	Ps. 31. 21.
He heard me, and delivered me	Ps. 34. 4; 120. 1.
He inclined unto me	Ps. 40. 1.
He brought me up out of an horrible pit	Ps. 40. 2.
He hath inclined His ear unto me	Ps. 116. 2.
He hath not given me over unto death	Ps. 118. 18.
He brought me to the banqueting-house	Song of Sol. 2. 4.
He loved me, and gave Himself for me	Gal. 2. 20.
He delivereth me	Ps. 18. 48.
He maketh me to lie down in green pastures	Ps. 23. 2.
He leadeth me beside the still waters ... in the paths of righteousness	Ps. 23. 2, 3.
He shall hide me	Ps. 27. 5.
He shall set me up upon a rock	Ps. 27. 5.

HUMILITY.

Thou shalt remember all the way the Lord thy God led thee, to humble thee	Deut. 8. 2, 3.
That He might humble thee	Deut. 8. 16.
He shall save the humble person	Job 22. 29.
He forgetteth not the cry of the humble	Ps. 9. 12.
Thou hast heard the desire of the humble	Ps. 10. 17.
Thou wilt prepare their heart, &c.	Ps. 10. 17.
Better it is to be of an humble spirit, &c.	Prov. 16. 19.
Honour shall uphold the humble in spirit	Prov. 29. 23.
I dwell with him that is of a contrite and humble spirit	Isa. 57. 15.
Humble yourselves	Jas. 4. 10; 1 Pet. 5. 6.
God giveth grace unto the humble	Jas. 4. 6; 1 Pet. 5. 5.
If my people shall humble themselves, and pray If their hearts be humbled, then will I remember My covenant	2 Chron. 7. 14. Lev. 26. 41, 42.
Because thou hast humbled thyself, I also have heard thee	2 Kings 22. 19.
Thou didst humble thyself } I have even heard Thou humbledst thyself } thee also	2 Chron. 34. 27.
The princes of Israel and the king humbled themselves, and when the Lord saw that they humbled themselves, &c.	2 Chron. 12. 6, 7.
Divers of them humbled themselves	Chron. 30. 11.
Hezekiah humbled himself for the pride of his heart	2 Chron. 32. 26.
When he was in affliction, he humbled himself greatly, and He was entreated of him	2 Chron. 33. 12, 13.
Thou hast not humbled thine heart	Dan. 5. 22.
Whosoever therefore shall humble himself as this little child, the same is greatest in the kingdom of heaven	Matt. 18. 4.
He that humbleth himself shall be exalted	Matt. 23. 12; Luke 14. 11.
Put on humbleness of mind	Col. 3. 12.
Before honour is humility	Prov. 15. 33; 18. 12.
By humility and the fear of the Lord are riches, and honour, and life	Prov. 22. 4.
Be clothed with humility	1 Pet. 5. 5.
Christ humbled Himself	Phil. 2. 8.
Walk humbly with thy God. ("Humble thyself to walk"—margin)	Micah 6. 8; Prov. 6. 3.

BACKSLIDING.

My sheep shall never perish, neither shall any pluck them out of My hand	John 10. 28; Heb. 13. 5.
Since I spake against him, I do earnestly remember him still	Jer. 31. 20.
Return, ye backsliding children, I will heal your backslidings	Jer. 3. 22; Mal. 3. 7.
Come, and let us return unto the Lord: for He hath torn, and He will heal us	Hosea 6. 1; Jer. 3. 22 (end).
Return unto the Lord . . . to our God, for He will abundantly pardon	Isa. 55. 7; Hos. 14. 1.
I will heal their backsliding, I will love them freely	Hosea 14. 4.
Do Thou it *for Thy Name's sake*, for our backslidings are many	Jer. 14. 7; Heb. 7. 25.
I will look unto the Lord . . . when I fall, I shall arise	Micah 7. 7, 8; Ps. 37. 24.

EXAMPLES OF BACKSLIDERS RESTORED.

David	2 Sam. 12. 13.
Peter	Mark 16. 7.
Prodigal Son	Luke 15. 20.
Behold, I stand at the door, and knock: if any man open the door, I will come in to him, &c.	Rev. 3. 20; Song of Sol. 5. 2.
My son, give Me thine *heart*	Prov. 23. 26.

but contrast Prov. 14. 14.

LEARN.

Learn of Me	Matt. 11. 29.
„ to fear Me	Deut. 4. 10.
„ to keep, and do	Deut. 5. 1.
„ Thy statutes	Ps. 119. 71.
„ to do well	Isa. 1. 17.
„ righteousness	Isa. 26. 9.
„ what that meaneth, &c.	Matt. 9. 13.
„ not to think above what is written	1 Cor. 4. 6.
„ first to show piety at home	1 Tim. 5. 4
"I have learned, in whatsoever state I am, therewith to be content"	Phil. 4. 11.

THE TITLE ON THE CROSS.

In Matthew . This is Jesus, the King of the Jews — Matt. 27. 37.
In Mark . . The King of the Jews . . Mark 15. 26.
In Luke . . This is the King of the Jews . Luke 23. 38.
In John . . Jesus of Nazareth, the King of
    the Jews . . . John 19. 19.

FULL TITLE.

"THIS IS JESUS OF NAZARETH, THE KING OF THE JEWS."
No contradiction in any of the four Gospels.

"IT IS FINISHED."

Sin, when *it is finished*, bringeth forth death . James 1. 15.
Jesus said, *It is finished* . . . and gave up the
    ghost . . . . . John 19. 30.

See 2 Cor. 5. 21.

COMMANDS AND INVITATIONS.

Call upon—unto Me	Ps. 50. 15; Jer. 33. 3.
Look unto Me	Isa. 45. 22.
Hearken unto Me	Isa. 51. 1, 4, 7.
Seek ye Me	Amos 5. 4.
Come unto Me	Matt. 11. 28.
Learn of Me	Matt. 11. 29.
Watch with Me	Matt. 26. 38.
Rejoice with Me	Luke 15. 6, 9.
Abide in Me	John 15. 4
Follow thou Me	John 21. 22.

"I WILL NOT."

I will not sit with the wicked . . Ps. 26. 5; 101. 4.
I will not fear what flesh can do unto me . Ps. 56. 4.
I will not forget Thy word . . Ps. 119. 16.
I will not be ashamed . . . Ps. 119. 46.

I will trust, and not be afraid . . Isa. 12. 2.

"ETERNAL LIFE"

Is the gift of God	Rom. 6. 23; 1 John 5. 11.
Is His promise	1 John 2. 25.
Is Jesus Christ	1 John 1. 2; 5. 20.
Is the gift of Christ	John 10. 28; 17. 2.
Is the result of believing	John 3. 15, 16, 36; 6. 47.
Is found in the Scriptures	John 5. 39.
Is to know the only true God, &c.	John 17. 3.
Is the result of denying oneself for Christ's sake	Mark 10. 30.
Is the portion of the righteous	Matt. 25. 46.
Whoso drinketh My blood, &c., hath eternal life	John 6. 54.
Ordained to eternal life	Acts 13. 48.
We are to know that we have it	1 John 5. 13.
We are to look for it	Jude 21.
Lay hold on eternal life	1 Tim. 6. 12, 19.

THE FEAR OF THE LORD

Is clean, enduring for ever	Ps. 19. 9.
That is wisdom	Job 28. 28.
Is the beginning of wisdom	Ps. 111. 10: Prov. 9. 10.
Is the beginning of knowledge	Prov. 1. 7.
Is to hate evil	Prov. 8. 13.
Prolongeth days	Prov. 10. 27.
In it is strong confidence	Prov. 14. 26.
Is a fountain of life	Prov. 14. 27.
Better is a little with it, than great treasure	Prov. 15. 16.
By it men depart from evil	Prov. 16. 6.
Tendeth to life	Prov. 19. 23.
By it are riches, and honour, and life	Prov. 22. 4.
Choose the fear of the Lord	Prov. 1. 29.
Be thou in fear of the Lord all the day long	Prov. 23. 17.

THE CITIES OF REFUGE

AS REPRESENTING THE LORD JESUS.

Num. 35. 6, 13, 14; Deut. 4. 41-43; Josh. 20. 2-9.

Kedesh = holy, holiness. Christ the Holy One. Christ of God is made unto us sanctification. 1 Cor. 1. 30; John 17. 19; Heb. 2. 11.

Shechem = shoulder, or that which bears or carries: a word implying strength. Christ has borne our sorrows, and sin. He bears rule as our King; the keys of government have been laid upon His shoulder. Ps. 55. 22; Isa. 9. 6; 53. 4-6; John 1. 29.

Hebron = fellowship, from a root meaning to join and bind together. 1 John 1. 3, 7; 1 Cor. 1. 9; 12. 12.

Bezer = stronghold, a rock, a fortress. Nahum 1. 7. Christ alone our Refuge. Prov. 18. 10; Isa. 32. 1, 2.

Ramoth = exaltation. Acts 2. 33; Phil. 2. 9; Eph. 2. 6.

Golan = joy. The Lord Jesus the only "morning without clouds." 2 Sam. 23. 4; Rom. 5. 11; Phil. 4. 4.

"CLEAN."

If I wash myself with snow-water, and make my hands never so clean, yet shalt Thou plunge me in the ditch	Job 9. 30, 31.
Who can bring a clean thing out of an unclean?	Job 14. 4.
What is man, that he should be clean?	Job 15. 14.
The heavens are not clean in His sight	Job 15. 15.
How can he be clean, that is born of a woman?	Job 25. 4.
All the ways of man are clean in his own eyes	Prov. 16. 2.
Who can say, I have made my heart clean?	Prov. 20. 9.
Purge me with hyssop, and I shall be clean: wash me, and I shall be whiter than snow	Ps. 51. 7.
Create in me a clean heart, O God.	Ps. 51. 10.
Wash you, make you clean	Isa. 1. 16.
O Jerusalem, wilt thou not be made clean?	Jer. 13. 27.
Then will I sprinkle clean water upon you, and ye shall be clean	Ezek. 36. 25.
Now ye are clean through My word	John 15. 3; Eph. 5. 26.
The fear of the Lord is clean	Ps. 19. 9.
Be ye clean, that bear the vessels of the Lord	Isa. 52. 11.
He that is washed is clean every whit	John 13. 10.
Arrayed in fine linen, clean and white	Rev. 19. 8.

HE CLEANSETH FROM

Secret faults	Ps. 19. 12.
Sin	Ps. 51. 2.
All iniquity	Jer. 33. 8.
All your filthiness	Ezek. 36. 25.
All your idols	Ezek. 36. 25; 37. 23.
All sin	1 John 1. 7.
All unrighteousness	1 John 1. 9.
"Having therefore these promises, let us cleanse ourselves"	2 Cor. 7. 1

READY.

All things are ready	Matt. 22. 4.
The wedding is ready	Matt. 22. 8.
Therefore be ye also ready	Matt. 24. 44.
They that were ready went in	Matt. 25. 10.
I am ready to die for the name of Jesus	Acts 21. 13.
I am ready to preach the gospel	Rom. 1. 15.
I am now ready to be offered	2 Tim. 4. 6.
Be ready to every good work	Titus 3. 1.
Be ready always to give an answer	1 Peter 3. 15.
God is ready to pardon	Neh. 9. 17.
,, to forgive	Ps. 86. 5.
,, to save	Isa. 38. 20.

GODLY SERVANTS.

Eliezer	Gen. 15. 2, with ch. 24.
Joseph	Gen. 39. 1-4, 9, 21, 23.
Obadiah	1 Kings 18. 3, 12.
The little maid	2 Kings 5. 2, 3.
Nehemiah	Nehem. 1. 11.
Daniel	Dan. 1. 8, 12.
The centurion's servant	Luke 7. 2, 8.
Phœbe	Rom. 16. 1, 2.
Onesimus	Philem. 10, 16.
Moses	Heb. 3. 5.

"FAITHFUL" MEN.

Abraham	Neh. 9. 8; Gal. 3. 9.
Moses	Heb. 3. 2, 5.
Samuel (margin)	1 Sam. 3. 20.
David	1 Sam. 22. 14.
Hananiah	Neh. 7. 2.
Timothy	1 Cor. 4. 17.
Tychicus	Eph. 6. 21.
Epaphras	Col. 1. 7.
Onesimus	Col. 4. 9.
Silvanus	1 Peter 5. 12.
Antipas	Rev. 2. 13.
Christ	Heb. 2. 17; 3. 2.

See also Matt. 24. 45; 25. 21, 23; and Rev. 2. 10.

PROMISES TO THE FAITHFUL.

The Lord preserveth the faithful	Ps. 31. 23.
Mine eyes shall be upon the faithful, that they may dwell with Me	Ps. 101. 6.
A faithful man shall abound with blessings	Prov. 28. 20.
Faithful over a few things . . . ruler over many	Matt. 25. 21.
Well done, good and faithful servant . . . enter thou into the joy of thy Lord	Matt. 25. 23.
Be thou faithful unto death, and I will give thee a crown of life	Rev. 2. 10.
They that are with Him are . . . faithful	Rev. 17. 14.
"He is faithful that promised"	Heb. 10. 23.

"FAITHFUL SAYINGS."

"Christ Jesus came . . . to save sinners"	1 Tim. 1. 15.
"Godliness is profitable unto all things"	1 Tim. 4. 8, 9.
"If we be dead with Him, we shall also live . . . if we suffer, we shall also reign with Him," &c.	2 Tim. 2. 11-13.
Believers—"be careful to maintain good works"	Titus 3. 8.

EMMANUEL—"GOD WITH US."

If God will be with me	Gen. 28. 20.
The God of my father hath been with me	Gen. 31. 5.
Forbear from meddling with God, who is with me	2 Chron. 35. 21.
When the Almighty was yet with me	Job 29. 5.
Thou art with me	Ps. 23. 4.
The Lord is with me as a mighty terrible One	Jer. 20. 11.
Notwithstanding the Lord stood with me, and strengthened me	2 Tim. 4. 17.

WE WITH GOD.

The faithful of the land may dwell with Me	Ps. 101. 6.
He walked with Me in peace and equity	Mal. 2. 6.
Tarry ye here, and watch with Me	Matt. 26. 38.
Could ye not watch with Me one hour?	Matt. 26. 40.
Ye are they which have continued with Me	Luke 22. 28.
To-day shalt thou be with Me in paradise	Luke 23. 43.
Ye have been with Me from the beginning	John 15. 27.
Father, I will that they also be with Me where I am	John 17. 24.
They shall walk with Me in white	Rev. 3. 4.
"He with Me." "Sit with Me in My throne"	Rev. 3. 20, 21.
"He that is not with Me is against Me"	Matt. 12. 30.
"Without Me ye can do nothing"	John 15. 5

EZRA'S GENEALOGY.

Ezra 7. 3.	Amariah,	The excellency of the Lord	Ps. 8. 1, 9; Isa. 28. 29.
Ezra 7. 2.	Ahitub,	A brother of goodness	Prov. 17. 17; 18. 24; Matt. 12. 46, 50.
Ezra 7. 2.	Zadok,	The justified one	Rom. 3. 24–26.
Ezra 7. 2.	Shallum,	The perfect one	Heb. 7. 28 (margin); 10. 14; 13. 21.
Ezra 7. 1.	Hilkiah,	God is my portion	Ps. 73. 26; Lam. 3. 24.
Ezra 7. 1.	Azariah,	One who hears God	Pro. 8. 34; Jno. 10. 27.
Ezra 7. 1.	Seraiah,	A prince of the Lord	1 Pet. 2. 9; Rev. 1. 5, 6.
EZRA		A Helper	2 Cor. 6. 1.

LOVE TO GOD,
SHEWN BY KEEPING HIS COMMANDMENTS.

If ye love Me, keep My commandments	John 14. 15.
He that hath My commandments, and keepeth them, he it is that loveth Me	John 14. 21.
If a man love Me, he will keep My words	John 14. 23.
If ye keep My commandments, ye shall abide in My love	John 15. 10.
Whoso keepeth His word, in him verily is the love of God perfected	1 John 2. 5.
This is the love of God, that we keep His commandments	1 John 5. 3.

DANIEL, A REPRESENTATION OF THE LORD.

His name (God my Judge)	Dan. 1. 6; John 8. 16-18.
Filled with wisdom	Dan. 1. 4; Isa. 11. 2; Luke 2. 40.
Without blemish	Dan. 1. 4; 1 Peter 1. 19
Would not defile himself	Dan. 1. 8; Heb. 7. 26.
God brought him into favour	Dan. 1. 9; Luke 2. 52.
Was better than all	Dan. 1. 20; Mark 7. 37; John 7. 46.
They sought to kill him	Dan. 2. 13; Luke 22. 2.
Secret revealed unto him	Dan. 2. 19; John 5. 20.
Praying before his God	Dan. 6. 10, 11; Mark 1. 35; 14. 35.
Cast into the den—raised up	Dan. 6. 16, 17, 23; Mat. 27.66; Acts 2. 26-32.
Go thy way, till the end be	Dan. 12. 13; Heb. 10. 12, 13, 37.

THE LORD KNOWETH

The way that I take	Job 23. 10.
The way of the righteous	Ps. 1. 6.
Our frame	Ps. 103. 14.
My down-sitting and up-rising ... my words	Ps. 139. 1-4.
Them that trust in Him	Nahum 1. 7.
That ye have need of all these things	Matt. 6. 32.
His sheep	John 10. 14, 27.
Them that are His	2 Tim. 2. 19.
How to deliver the godly out of temptations	2 Peter 2. 9.

PROMISES TO THE UPRIGHT.

God's countenance beholds the upright	Ps. 11. 7.
God shows Himself upright to the upright man	Ps. 18. 25.
God knoweth the days of the upright	Ps. 37. 18.
God directeth the way of the upright	Prov. 21. 29.
God withholds no good thing from them that walk uprightly	Ps. 84. 11.
God is a buckler to them that walk uprightly	Prov. 2. 7.
Gladness is sown for the upright	Ps. 97. 11.
The generation of the upright shall be blessed	Ps. 112. 2.
Unto the upright there ariseth light in darkness	Ps. 112. 4.
The tabernacle of the upright shall flourish	Prov. 14. 11.
The upright shall have good things in possession	Prov. 28. 10.
The upright shall dwell in the land	Prov. 2. 21.
,, ,, Thy presence	Ps. 140. 13.
Behold the upright: the end of that man is peace	Ps. 37. 37.

THOSE WHO SAID, "MY GOD."

Jacob	Gen. 28. 21.
Moses	Exod. 15. 2.
Ruth	Ruth 1. 16.
David	1 Chron. 28. 20.
Elijah	1 Kings 17. 21.
Micaiah	2 Chron. 18. 13.
Nehemiah	Neh. 5. 19.
Isaiah	Isa. 7. 13.
Daniel	Dan. 6. 22.
Jonah	Jonah 2. 6.
Micah	Micah 7. 7.
Thomas	John 20. 28.
Paul	Rom. 1. 8.
Our Lord	Matt. 27. 46; John 20. 17.

GOD'S COMMANDS (TO HOUSEHOLDS).

IN THE NEW TESTAMENT.

WIVES, submit to your husbands, as unto the Lord ... reverence your husbands.	Eph. 5. 22, 33.
,, submit to your husbands, as it is fit in the Lord	Col. 3. 18.
,, be obedient to your husbands, that the word of God be not blasphemed	Titus 2. 5.
HUSBANDS, love your wives, even as Christ also loved the Church ... even as yourselves	Eph. 5. 25, 33.
,, dwell with your wives according to knowledge, that your prayers be not hindered	1 Peter 3, 7.
FATHERS, bring your children up in the nurture and admonition of the Lord	Eph. 6. 4.
,, provoke not your children, lest they be discouraged	Col. 3. 21.
CHILDREN, obey your parents in the Lord: for this is right	Eph. 6. 1.
,, obey your parents in all things: for this is well-pleasing unto the Lord	Col. 3. 20.
,, shew piety (margin) at home; for that is good and acceptable before God	1 Tim. 5. 4.
MASTERS, forbear threatening: knowing that your Master also is in heaven	Eph. 6. 9.
,, give unto servants what is just and equal; knowing that ye also have a Master in heaven	Col. 4. 1.
SERVANTS, be obedient, as unto Christ	Eph. 6. 5.
,, as the servants of Christ, doing the will of God from the heart	Eph. 6. 6, 7.
,, obey in singleness of heart, fearing God	Col. 3. 22.
,, whatsoever ye do, do heartily, as to the Lord, and not unto men; for ye serve the Lord Christ	Col. 3. 23, 24.
,, count your masters worthy of honour, that the name of God and His doctrine be not blasphemed	1 Tim. 6. 1.
,, adorn the doctrine of God our Saviour in all things	Titus 2. 10, with 9.

WHEN YOU HAVE CROSSED JORDAN

Beware of idolatry	Deut. 4. 15-24.
Destroy the Lord's enemies	Deut. 25. 19.
Love the Lord, obey His voice, cleave unto Him; for He is thy life	Deut. 30. 20.
Beware lest thine heart be lifted up, and thou forget the Lord thy God	Deut. 8. 11, 14.
Honour and obey God's word	Deut. 6. 1, 2.
Be not unequally yoked together with unbelievers	Deut. 7. 1-3.
Take heed to yourself, that your heart be not deceived, &c.	Deut. 11. 16.
Be upright, just, and honest	Deut. 19. 14 to end.
Exercise brotherly-kindness and charity	Deut. 15. 7, 8.
Keep the feasts of the Lord	Deut. 16. 6, 9, 13; with 1 Cor. 5. 8.
Give the first-fruits to God	Deut. 26. 1, 2.

THE HEART OF THE LORD.

It grieved Him at His heart	Gen. 6. 6.
The Lord said in His heart, &c.	Gen. 8. 21.
If He set His heart upon man	Job 34. 14.
A man after His own heart	1 Sam. 13. 14.
According to His own heart	2 Sam. 7. 21; 1 Chron. 17. 19.
Mine heart shall be there perpetually	1 Kings 9. 3; 2 Chron. 7. 16.
Thou hast ravished My heart	Song of Sol. 4. 9.
The day of vengeance is in Mine heart	Isa. 63. 4.
I will give you pastors according to Mine heart	Jer. 3. 15.
I am pained at My very heart, &c.	Jer. 4. 19.
Neither came it into Mine heart	Jer. 7. 31.
Until He have performed the intents of His heart	Jer. 30. 24.
Assuredly with My whole heart	Jer. 32. 41.
Mine heart is turned within Me	Hosea 11. 8.
Then did My heart rejoice	Acts 2. 26.
Learn of Me; for I am meek and lowly in heart	Matt. 11. 29.

BENEDICTIONS
(NEW TESTAMENT).

The God of peace be with you all	Rom. 15. 33.
The grace of our Lord Jesus Christ be with you	Rom. 16. 20.
My love be with you all in Christ Jesus	1 Cor. 16. 24.
The God of love and peace shall be with you	2 Cor. 13. 11.
The grace of the Lord Jesus Christ, and the love of God, and the communion of the Holy Ghost, be with you all	2 Cor. 13. 14.
Grace be with you—with thee	Col. 4. 18; 1 Tim. 6. 21.
The Lord of peace ... be with you all	2 Thess. 3. 16; with Phil. 4. 7.
Peace be with you all that are in Christ Jesus	1 Peter 5. 14; John 20. 19, 21, 26.

BEAUTY.

"The beauty of the Lord"	Ps. 27. 4.
"So shall the King greatly desire thy beauty"	Ps. 45. 11.
"The beauty of the Lord our God be upon us"	Ps. 90. 17.
"Worship the Lord in the beauty of holiness"	Ps. 96. 9, 6.
"Thine eyes shall see the King in His beauty"	Isa. 33. 17.
"How great is His beauty!"	Zech. 9. 17.
"He will beautify the meek with salvation"	Ps. 149. 4.

WHITE AS SNOW
(GOD, AND ALL HIS).

"Her Nazarites were purer than snow"	Lam. 4. 7.
The Lord Jesus	Mark 9. 3.
His people	Ps. 51. 7.
Their sins	Isa. 1. 18.
The angel of the Lord	Matt. 28. 3.
The Son of man	Rev. 1. 14.
The Ancient of days	Dan. 7. 9.
If I wash myself with snow-water ... yet shalt Thou plunge me in the ditch, &c.	Job 9. 30, 31.

"WITH ME"

Dwell the faithful of the land . . . Ps. 101. 6.

PRECEPTS.

Here. { Gather . . . . . Matt. 12. 30.
Rejoice . . . . . Luke 15, 6, 9.
Watch . . . . . Matt. 26. 38, 40.

They shall be with Me where I am . . John 17. 24.

PROMISES.

There. { Walk . . . . . Rev. 3. 4.
Sup . . . . . Rev. 3. 20.
Sit . . . . . Rev. 3. 21.

JESUS OF NAZARETH.

JESUS SO CALLED BY.

Philip to Nathanael . . . . John 1. 45.
Man with an unclean spirit . . . Mark 1. 24.
Multitude (at Jericho) to blind Bartimæus . Luke 18. 37.
Multitude (at Jerusalem) to one another, "Jesus,
    the prophet of Nazareth" . . . Matt. 21. 11.
Band of men in the garden . . . John 18. 5, 7.
High priest's maid-servant to Peter . . Mark 14. 67.
Pilate (the title on the cross) . . . John 19. 19.
The angel to the women at the sepulchre . Mark 16. 6.
The two disciples . . . . Luke 24. 19.
Peter to the "men of Israel" . . . Acts 2. 22.
Peter to the impotent man, "Jesus Christ of
    Nazareth" . . . . . Acts 3. 6.
Peter to the rulers and elders, "Jesus Christ of
    Nazareth" . . . . . Acts 4. 10.
False witnesses (about Stephen) to the council . Acts 6. 14.
Peter to Cornelius . . . . Acts 10. 38.
Himself to Saul . . . . . Acts 22. 8.
Paul to Agrippa . . . . . Acts 26. 9.

"FORTY DAYS AND FORTY NIGHTS."

A SCRIPTURAL PERIOD OF TRIAL, ENDING IN VICTORY TO THE GOOD, AND IN RUIN TO THE EVIL.

Rain upon the earth in the flood	Gen. 7. 4, 12, 17.
The spies searched the land	Num. 13. 25; 14. 34.
Defiance of Israel by Goliath	1 Sam. 17, 16.
Ezekiel to bear the iniquity of the house of Judah	Ezek. 4. 6.
Time for Nineveh to repent	Jonah 3. 4.
The fasting of Moses	Deut. 9. 9, 18.
,, Elias	1 Kings 19. 8.
,, Christ	Matt. 4. 2.

In the history of our Lord, this period of forty days and forty nights occurs THREE times:

1. Period between His birth and presentation in the temple. Luke 3. 22; with Lev. 12.

2. Period of His fasting and temptation. Matt. 4. 2; Mark 1. 13; Luke 4. 2.

3. Period between His resurrection and ascension. Acts 1. 3.

"WELL-PLEASED"—"WELL-PLEASING."

(CONTRAST 1 COR. 10. 5.)

Well-pleased with Thy land	Ps. 85. 1 (margin).
Well-pleased for His righteousness' sake	Isa. 42. 21.
My beloved Son, in whom I am well-pleased	Matt. 3. 17; 12. 18; 17. 5; 2 Peter 1. 17.
With such sacrifices God is well-pleased	Heb. 13. 16.
A sacrifice well-pleasing to God	Phil. 4. 18.
Obey; for this is well-pleasing unto the Lord	Col. 3. 20.
Working in you that which is well-pleasing in His sight	Heb. 13. 21.

BORN OF GOD

The Father	John 1. 13; 1 John 3. 9.
The Son	1 John 2. 29, with v. 28.
The Spirit	John 3. 8.

AT THE FEET OF JESUS

The place of pardon	Luke 7. 38.
The place of healing	Matt. 15. 30.
The place of learning	Luke 10. 39; Deut. 33. 3.
The place of (successful) prayer	Mark 5. 22; 7. 25.
The place of thanksgiving	Luke 17. 16.
The place of rest	Luke 8. 35.
The place of comfort	John 11. 32.
The place of worship	Rev. 1. 17.

"ONE THING."

Not one thing hath failed	Joshua 23. 14.
One thing have I desired	Ps. 27. 4.
One thing befalleth all	Eccles. 3. 19.
One thing thou lackest	Mark 10. 21.
One thing is needful	Luke 10. 42.
One thing I know	John 9. 25.
This one thing I do	Phil. 3. 13.
Be not ignorant of this one thing	2 Peter 3. 8.

GOD (LIGHT—LOVE—LIFE).

As Father	Light	1 John 1. 5; Jas. 1. 17.
As Son	Love	John 15. 13; 1 John 3. 16.
As Holy Ghost	Life	Rom. 8. 2, 10; 2 Cor. 3. 6.

"IF ANY MAN"

(IN JOHN).

"Will do His will, he shall know of the doctrine	John 7. 17, with 10. 31.
"Thirst, let him come unto Me, and drink"	John 7. 37.
"Enter in, he shall be saved," &c.	John 10. 9.
"Serve Me, let Him follow Me," &c.	John 12. 26.

See also chap. 12. 47.

"HE WAS *BRUISED* FOR OUR INIQUITIES."

Gold was beaten for the cherubims	Exodus 25. 18.
Oil was beaten out for the light	Exodus 27. 20; Lev. 24. 2.
Incense was beaten very small—a perfume holy unto the Lord	Exod. 30, 35, 36.
Corn was beaten out for the meat-offering	Lev. 2. 14, 16.
Gold was beaten for the candlestick and its branches	Numb. 8. 4.

See Hebrews 8. 1, 2; 9. 11, 12.

"SACRIFICES OF THANKSGIVING."
LEV. 7. 12, 13; 22. 29.

Offer unto God thanksgiving	Ps. 50. 14.
Whoso offereth praise glorifieth Me	Ps. 50. 23.
Let them sacrifice the sacrifices of thanksgiving, and declare His works with rejoicing (marg.)	Ps. 107. 22.
I will offer to Thee the sacrifice of thanksgiving	Ps. 116. 17.
I will sacrifice unto Thee with the voice of thanksgiving	Jonah 2. 9.
By Him therefore let us offer the sacrifice of praise to God continually... giving thanks to His name	Heb. 13. 15, 16.

Contrast Amos 4, 5.

WHO MAY "GIVE THANKS"?

The living	Ps. 119. 175; Isa. 38. 19.
The forgiven	Isa. 12. 1; Ps. 51. 15.
The upright	Ps. 33. 1.
They that seek the Lord	Ps. 22. 26.
The poor and needy	Ps. 74. 21.
The babes and sucklings	Matt. 21. 16.
His saints	Ps. 149. 1, 5, 6, 9.
His servants, that fear Him	Rev. 19. 5.

See also Psalm 150.

"FROM WHENCE COMETH MY HELP?"

My help cometh from the Lord . . . Ps. 121. 2.

PAST.

Thou hast been my help . . . . Ps. 27. 9.
He helped me . . . . . Ps. 116. 6.
The Lord helped me . . . . Ps. 118. 13.

PRESENT.

God is mine helper . . . . Ps. 54. 4.
Thou art my help . . . . Ps. 40. 17; 70. 5.
I am helped . . . . . Ps. 28. 7.

FUTURE

The Lord God will help me . . . Isa. 50. 7, 9.
Fear not, I will help thee . , . Isa. 41. 10, 13, 14.

therefore Psalm 63. 7.

MEANING OF THE NAMES OF THE TWELVE CAPTAINS OF THE TRIBES.

NUMBERS 2.

Of the tribe of	Judah .	Nahshon .	Diviner.
,,	Issachar .	Nethaneel .	Gift of God.
,,	Zebulun .	Eliab .	My God, my Father.
,,	Reuben .	Elizur .	My God, my Rock.
,,	Simeon .	Shelumiel .	God is my Peace.
,,	Gad .	Eliasaph .	God hath added.
,,	Ephraim .	Elishama .	My God hears.
,,	Manasseh .	Gamaliel .	God is my reward.
,,	Benjamin .	Abidan .	My Father is Judge.
,,	Dan .	Ahiezer .	My brother is Help.
,,	Asher .	Pagiel .	God is my Advocate.
,,	Napthali .	Ahira .	Brother of iniquity.

PREPARATION.

Prepare to meet thy God	Amos 4. 12.
Prepare your hearts unto the Lord, and serve Him only .	1 Sam. 7. 3.
Lord, Thou hast heard the desire of the humble: Thou wilt prepare their heart	Ps. 10. 17.
The preparation of the heart is from the Lord .	Prov. 16. 1.
If a man purge himself from these, he shall be a vessel unto honour, . . . prepared unto every good work	2 Tim. 2. 21.
Eye hath not seen, nor ear heard . . . the things which God hath prepared for them that love Him .	1 Cor. 2. 9.
He hath prepared for them a city .	Heb. 11. 16.
In My Father's house are many mansions . . . I go to prepare a place for you	John 14. 2, 3.
Then shall the King say unto them on His right hand, Come, ye blessed of My Father, inherit the kingdom prepared for you	Matt. 25. 34.
Then shall He also say to them on the left hand, Depart, ye cursed, into everlasting fire, prepared for the devil and his angels .	Matt. 25. 41.
I John saw the holy city, new Jerusalem . . . prepared as a bride adorned for her husband	Rev. 21. 2.

"IN GOD."

Psalm 62. 7.

"IN GOD
　　　my Salvation,
　　　　　my Glory,
　　　　　　　my Strength,
　　　　　　　　　my Refuge,
　　　　　　　　　　　IN GOD."

Therefore "Trust IN HIM at all times," verse 8.

THE SECOND COMING OF THE LORD
(THE BELIEVER'S HOPE).

I will come again, and receive you unto Myself	John 14. 3.
This same Jesus shall so come in like manner	Acts 1. 11.
Waiting for the coming of our Lord Jesus	1 Cor. 1. 7.
We shall not all sleep, but all be changed	1 Cor. 15. 51, 52.
To wait for His Son from heaven	1 Thess. 1. 10.
The Lord Himself shall descend with a shout	1 Thess. 4. 16 to end.
He shall come to be glorified in His saints	2 Thess. 1. 10.
A crown of righteousness . . . at that day	2 Tim. 4. 8.
Looking for that blessed hope, &c.	Titus 2. 13; Phil. 3. 20.
Unto them that look for Him, shall He appear	Heb. 9. 28.
He that shall come will come, and not tarry	Heb. 10. 37; with 2 Peter 3 9.
Found unto praise . . . at the appearing	1 Peter 1. 7.
Abide in Him . . . not ashamed at His coming	1 John 2. 28.
When He shall appear, we shall be like Him	1 John 3. 2; Col. 3. 4.
The Lord cometh with ten thousand of His saints	Jude 14; with 1 Thess. 3. 13.
Behold, I come quickly	Rev. 3. 11; Rev. 22. 7, 12, 20.

"MUST."

Ye must be born again	John 3. 7; see also verse 14.
God is a Spirit: and they that worship Him must worship Him in spirit and in truth	John 4. 24.
He that cometh to God must believe	Heb. 11. 6.
There is none other name under heaven, whereby we must be saved	Acts 4. 12.
We must through much tribulation enter into the kingdom of God	Acts 14. 22.
The servant of the Lord must not strive	2 Tim. 2. 24.
Wherefore ye must needs be subject	Rom. 13. 5.
For we must all appear before the judgment-seat of Christ	2 Cor. 5. 10; with Rom 14. 10.

WAITING.

"Blessed are all they that wait for Him"	Isa. 30. 18.
Wait on the Lord—upon Me	Ps. 27. 14; Zeph. 3. 8.
I wait on Thee	Ps. 25. 21.
My soul waiteth upon God	Ps. 62. 1.
I will wait upon the Lord	Isa. 8. 17.
I will wait on Thy name	Ps. 52. 9.
These wait all upon Thee	Ps. 104. 27.
Our eyes wait upon the Lord our God	Ps. 123. 2.
The eyes of all wait upon Thee	Ps. 145. 15.
We will wait upon Thee	Jer. 14. 22.

"WHAT WAIT I FOR?"
PSALM 39. 7.

For the Lord	Ps. 130. 5; 33. 20.
For my God	Ps. 69. 3.
For the God of my salvation	Micah 7. 7.
For His salvation	Gen. 49. 18.
For His strength	Ps. 59. 9.
For the coming of our Lord	1 Cor. 1. 7; Luke 12. 36.
For His Son from heaven	1 Thess. 1. 10.

SHOULD I WAIT ANY LONGER?

Wait patiently	Ps. 37. 7; Ps. 40. 1; 2 Thess. 3. 5.
Wait quietly	Lam. 3. 26.
Wait continually	Hosea 12. 6.
Wait only	Ps. 62. 5.
Wait all the day	Ps. 25. 5.
Wait at the posts of My doors	Prov. 8. 34.
Wait without being ashamed	Ps 25. 3; Isa. 49. 23.

Heb. 10. 36, 37.

PROMISES TO WAITING.

Salvation	Prov. 20.22; Isa. 25. 9.
Sustenance	Ps. 145. 15.
Strength	Ps. 27. 14.
Renewal of strength	Isa. 40. 31.
An inheritance	Ps. 37. 9, 34.
No (fear, or) shame	Isa. 49. 23.
The Lord's goodness	Lam. 3. 25, 26.

Prov. 27. 18; Isa. 30. 18.

HIS VOICE.

It is a still small voice	1 Kings 19. 12.
It is a mighty voice	Ps. 68. 33.
It is sweet	Song of Sol. 2. 14.
It is glorious	Isa. 30. 30.
It is like the voice of a multitude	Dan. 10. 6.
It is as the sound of many waters	Rev. 1. 15.

WE SHOULD HEAR HIS VOICE

Diligently	Exodus 15. 26.
Obediently	Deut. 4. 30.
Carefully	Deut. 15. 5.
Attentively	Job 37. 2.
To-day	Heb. 3. 7, 13, 15.

EFFECT OF HEARING HIS VOICE.

We keep His commandments	Deut. 13. 18.
We rejoice greatly	John 3. 29.
We know His voice	John 10. 4.
We follow Him	John 10. 4, 27.
We become His witnesses	Acts 22. 14, 15.

CARES (ANXIOUS THOUGHTS).

Hinder watchfulness for the Lord's return	Luke 21. 34.
"Choke the Word," rendering it unfruitful	Matt. 13. 22.
Prevent perfect development of "the seed"	Luke 8. 14.

"TAKE NO THOUGHT"

For your life . . . nor yet for your body	Matt. 6. 25.
For raiment	Matt. 6. 28.
For food	Matt. 6. 31.
For the morrow	Matt. 6. 34.
For your words (when you are delivered up)	Matt. 10. 19.

LAWFUL CARES.

For the things of the Lord, how we may please the Lord	1 Cor. 7. 32.
Care one for another	1 Cor. 12. 25.
Care (in a measure in fellowship with Christ) of the churches	2 Cor. 11. 28.

"CASTING ALL YOUR CARE UPON HIM."

For He careth for you	1 Peter 5. 7.
Live not in careful suspense (margin)	Luke 12. 29.
I would have you without carefulness	1 Cor. 7. 32.
Not careful in the year of drought	Jer. 17. 8.
Not careful to answer	Dan. 3. 16.

BE CAREFUL FOR NOTHING; but in everything by prayer and supplication, with thanksgiving, let your requests be made known unto God. Phil. 4. 6.

And the peace of God, which passeth all understanding, shall keep your hearts and minds through Christ Jesus.

STONES ROLLED AWAY.

"Who shall roll us away the stone?"
"When they looked, they saw that the stone *was* rolled away: for it was very great."—MARK xvi. 3, 4.

THE STONE ROLLED AWAY.
GENESIS.

The serpent beguiled me, and I did eat. (iii. 13.)

A flaming sword . . . to keep the way of the tree of life. (iii. 24.)

The waters prevailed exceedingly upon the earth . . . and every living substance was destroyed. (vii. 19, 23.)

The water was spent in the bottle, and she cast the child under one of the shrubs. (xxi. 15.)

What wilt Thou give me, seeing I go childless? (xv. 2.)

The Son of God was manifested, that He might destroy the works of the devil.
(1 John iii. 8.)
I am come that they might have life, and that they might have it more abundantly.
(John x. 10.)
I am the . . . life. (Jn. xiv. 6.)

The face of the ground was dry . . . the earth was dried . . . the Lord said, Neither will I again smite any more every living thing, as I have done.
(viii. 13, 14, 21.)
God opened her eyes, and she saw a well of water; and she went, and filled the bottle with water, and gave the lad drink. (xxi. 19.)

Sarah . . . bare Abraham a son in his old age. (xxi. 2.)

THE STONE ROLLED AWAY.

GENESIS—continued.

Take now thy son, thine only son Isaac, whom thou lovest . . . and offer him for a burnt offering. (xxii. 2.)

Behold behind him a ram . . . Abraham offered him up for a burnt offering in the stead of his son. (xxii. 13.)

Jacob was greatly afraid and distressed. (xxxii. 7.)

Esau ran to meet him, and embraced him. (xxxiii. 4.)

They took Joseph, and cast him into a pit . . . they sold Joseph to the Ishmeelites . . . they sold him into Egypt. (xxxvii. 24, 28, 36.)

Pharaoh said unto Joseph, See, I have set thee over all the land of Egypt. Joseph's brethren bowed down themselves before him. (xli. 41; xlii. 6.)

EXODUS.

The Egyptians made the children of Israel to serve with rigour. The children of Israel sighed by reason of the bondage. (i. 13; ii. 23.)

The Lord saved Israel . . . out of the hand of the Egyptians; and Israel saw the Egyptians dead upon the sea shore. There remained not so much as one of them. (xiv. 28, 30.)

The Egyptians pursued after them . . . and overtook them encamping by the sea. (xiv. 9.)

The children of Israel went into the midst of the sea upon the dry ground. (xiv. 22.)

Ye have brought us forth into this wilderness, to kill this whole assembly with hunger. (xvi. 3.)

This is the bread, which the Lord hath given you to eat. . . they gathered every man according to his eating. (xvi. 15, 18.)

LEVITICUS.

Their transgressions in all their sins. (xvi. 16.)

The goat shall bear . . . all their iniquities. . . Clean from all your sins. (xvi. 22, 30.)

THE STONE ROLLED AWAY.

NUMBERS.

The plague is begun. (xvi. 46.)

The plague was stayed. (xvi. 48, 50.)

There was no water for the congregation. (xx. 2.)

The water came out abundantly, and the congregation drank. (xx. 11.)

The Lord sent fiery serpents among the people, and they bit the people; and much people of Israel died. (xxi. 6.)

Moses made a serpent of brass, and set it upon a pole . . . if a serpent had bitten any man, when he beheld the serpent of brass, he lived. (xxi. 9.)

There we saw the giants, the sons of Anak. (xiii. 33.)

There was none of the Anakims left. (Joshua xi. 22.)

DEUTERONOMY.

Zamzummims; a people great, and many, and tall, as the Anakims. (ii. 20, 21.)

The Lord destroyed them before them . . . and they dwelt in their stead. (ii. 21.)

Sihon king of Heshbon would not let us pass. . . . Sihon came out against us, he and all his people. (ii. 30, 32.)

The Lord our God delivered him before us . . . we smote him . . . and all his people. . . . We took all his cities. . . . There was not one city too strong for us: the Lord our God delivered all unto us. (ii. 33, 34, 36.)

Og the king of Bashan came out against us, he and all his people. . . . All his cities were fenced with high walls, gates, and bars. (iii. 1, 5.)

The Lord our God delivered into our hands Og . . . and all his people. . . . We took all his cities . . . there was not a city which we took not. . . . And we utterly destroyed them.

(iii. 3, 4, 6.)

THE STONE ROLLED AWAY.

JOSHUA.

Jericho was straitly shut up . . . none went out, and none came in. (vi. 1.)

The wall fell down flat, so that the people went up into the city. (vi. 20.)

The men of Ai smote them . . . wherefore the hearts of the people melted. (vii. 5.)

Joshua burnt Ai, and made it an heap for ever. (viii. 28.)

All the kings . . . gathered themselves together to fight with Joshua and with Israel. (ix. 1, 2.)

All these kings . . . did Joshua take at one time, because the Lord God of Israel fought for Israel. (x. 42.)

They (the kings) went out, they and all their hosts with them, even as the sand that is upon the sea-shore in multitude fight against Israel. (xi. 4, 5.)

The Lord delivered them into the hand of Israel . . . and they smote them, until they left them none remaining (xi. 8.)

JUDGES.

Sisera gathered together all his chariots, even nine hundred chariots of iron, and all the people that were with him. (iv. 13.)

The Lord discomfited Sisera, and all his chariots, and all his host. (iv. 15.)

Midian prevailed against Israel . . . And they came as grasshoppers for multitude. (vi. 2, 5.)

All the host (of Midian) ran, and cried, and fled. . . . The Lord set every man's sword against his fellow. (vii. 21, 22.)

The children of Ammon passed over Jordan to fight against Judah, and . . . Benjamin, and . . . Ephraim; so that Israel was sore distressed. (x. 9.)

The Lord delivered them into his hands. . . . Thus the children of Ammon were subdued before the children of Israel. (xi. 32, 33.)

THE STONE ROLLED AWAY.

JUDGES—continued.

The Philistines took him (Samson), and put out his eyes, and bound him. (xvi. 21.)

The house fell upon the lords, and upon all the people. (xvi. 30.)

RUTH.

Call me Mara: for the Almighty hath dealt very bitterly with me. (i. 20.)

Blessed be the Lord, which hath not left thee this day without a kinsman. (iv. 14.)

I. SAMUEL.

Hannah had no child. (i. 5, 6.)

She bare a son, and called his name Samuel. (i. 20.)

The Philistines fought, and Israel was smitten. . . . And the ark of God was taken. (iv. 10, 11.)

The Philistines have brought again the ark of the Lord. . . . So the Philistines were subdued. (vi. 21, vii. 13.)

The Philistines drew near to battle against Israel. (vii. 10.)

The Lord thundered with a great thunder . . . and discomfited them. (vii. 10.)

There went out a champion out of the camp of the Philistines, named Goliath, of Gath. (xvii. 4.)

David prevailed over the Philistine . . . and smote the Philistine, and slew him. (xvii. 50.)

David said in his heart, I shall now perish one day by the hand of Saul. (xxvii. 1.)

Saul died . . . David reigned forty years. (xxxi. 6; 2 Sam. v. 4.)

The Amalekites had smitten Ziklag, and burned it with fire, and had taken the women captives. (xxx. 1, 2.)

David recovered all that the Amalekites had carried away: and David rescued his two wives. (xxx. 18.)

THE STONE ROLLED AWAY.

II. SAMUEL.

The Lord sent a pestilence upon Israel. (xxiv. 15.)

The Lord was entreated for the land, and the plague was stayed from Israel. (xxiv. 25.)

I. KINGS.

The son of the woman fell sick; and his sickness was so sore, there was no breath left in him. (xvii. 17.)

The soul of the child came into him again, and he revived. (xvii. 22.)

There shall not be dew nor rain these years . . . no rain in the land. (xvii. 1-7.)

There was a great rain. (xviii. 45.)

I, even I only, am left. Lord, take away my life. (xix. 4, 10, 14.)

Behold there appeared a chariot of fire . . . and Elijah went up by a whirlwind into heaven. 2 Kings ii. 11.

Ben-hadad . . . gathered all his host together, thirty and two kings with him, and horses, and chariots: and he went up and besieged Samaria, and warred against it. (xx. 1.)

Ben-hadad escaped on an horse . . . and the king of Israel went out, and smote the horses and chariots, and slew the Syrians with a great slaughter. (xx. 20, 21.)

The children of Israel pitched before them like two little flocks of kids; but the Syrians filled the country. (xx. 27.)

The children of Israel slew of the Syrians an hundred thousand footmen in one day. (xx. 29.)

II. KINGS.

The king of Moab rebelled against the king of Israel. (iii. 5.)

The Israelites rose up and smote the Moabites, so that they fled before them. (iii. 24.)

My husband is dead . . . and the creditor is come to take unto him my two sons to be bondmen. (iv. 1.)

Go, sell the oil, and pay thy debt, and live thou and thy children of the rest. (iv. 7.)

THE STONE ROLLED AWAY.

II. KINGS—continued.

She hath no child, and her husband is old. (iv. 14.)	The woman conceived, and bare a son. (iv. 17.)
He sat on her knees till noon, and then died. (iv. 20.)	The child opened his eyes. . . . She took up her son, and went out. (iv. 35, 37.)
There was a dearth in the land. (iv. 38.)	They did eat, and left thereof. (iv. 44.)
There is death in the pot. (iv. 40.)	There was no harm in the pot. (iv. 41.)
But he was a leper. (v. 1.)	His flesh came again like unto the flesh of a little child, and he was clean. (v. 14.)
The axe head fell into the water. (vi. 5.)	The iron did swim. (vi. 6.)
The king of Syria sent thither horses, and chariots, and a great host: and they came by night, and compassed the city about. (vi. 14.)	The Lord smote them with blindness. . . . So the bands of Syria came no more into the land of Israel. (vi. 18, 23.)
Ben-hadad . . . gathered all his host, and went up, and besieged Samaria. (vi. 24.)	The Syrians arose . . . left their tents . . . and fled for their life. (vii. 7.)
There was a great famine in Samaria. (vi. 25.)	A measure of fine flour was sold for a shekel, and two measures of barley for a shekel, according to the word of the Lord. (vii. 16.)
The king of Syria oppressed Israel. (xiii. 4.)	The Lord gave Israel a saviour, so that they went out from under the hand of the Syrians. (xiii. 5.)

THE STONE ROLLED AWAY.

II. KINGS—continued.

Sennacherib king of Assyria came up against all the fenced cities of Judah, and took them ... and with a great host against Jerusalem. (xviii. 13, 17.)

The angel of the Lord went out, and smote in the camp of the Assyrians an hundred fourscore and five thousand. ... So Sennacherib king of Assyria departed. (xix. 35, 36.)

Thou shalt die, and not live. (xx. 1.)

I will add unto thy days fifteen years. (xx. 6.)

He carried out thence all the treasures of the house of the Lord. ... He carried away all Jerusalem ... into captivity to Babylon. ... He burnt the house of the Lord.
(xxiv. 13–15 ; xxv. 9.)

They went up out of the captivity ... and came again unto Jerusalem. ... Take these vessels into the temple in Jerusalem, and let the house of God be builded. ... They builded, and finished it.
(Ezra ii. 1 ; v. 15 ; vi. 14.)

I. CHRONICLES.

The Philistines fought against Israel ; and the men of Israel fled. (x. i.)

David smote the Philistines, and subdued them. (xviii. 1.)

The children of Ammon hired the Syrians, and gathered themselves together to battle.
(xix. 6, 7.)

The children of Ammon ... fled. ... The Syrians fled before Israel. (xix. 15, 18.)

II. CHRONICLES.

Jeroboam came against Abijah with eight hundred thousand chosen men, mighty men of valour. (xiii. 3.)

God smote Jeroboam and all Israel before Abijah and Judah. And the children of Israel fled.
(xiii. 15, 16.)

There came out against them Zerah the Ethiopian with an host of a million, and three hundred chariots. (xiv. 9.)

The Lord smote the Ethiopians ... the Ethiopians fled. The Ethiopians were overthrown, that they could not recover themselves. (xiv. 12, 13.)

THE STONE ROLLED AWAY.

II. CHRONICLES—continued.

The captains of the chariots saw Jehoshaphat ... they compassed about him to fight. (xviii. 31.)

The Lord helped him; and God moved them from him. (xviii. 31.)

There came some that told Jehoshaphat, saying, There cometh a great multitude against thee. (xx. 2 with 12.)

They looked unto the multitude, and, behold, they were dead bodies fallen to the earth, and none escaped. (xx. 24.)

EZRA.

Then ceased the work of the house of God. (iv. 24.)

This house was finished. (vi. 15.)

The enemy in the way. (viii. 22.)

The hand of our God was upon us, and He delivered us from the hand of the enemy, and of such as lay in wait by the way. (viii. 31.)

NEHEMIAH.

The wall of Jerusalem also is broken down, and the gates thereof are burned with fire. (i. 3.)

So the wall was finished. . . . The wall was built, and I had set up the doors. (vi. 15, vii. 1.)

ESTHER.

The letters were sent ... to destroy, to kill, and to cause to perish, all Jews. (iii. 13.)

The Jews smote all their enemies. . . . Had rest from their enemies. . . . Had gladness and feasting, and a good day. (ix. 5, 16, 19.)

If I perish, I perish. (iv. 16.)

She obtained favour in his sight. (v. 2.)

THE STONE ROLLED AWAY.

ESTHER—*continued.*

Let a gallows be made . . . that Mordecai may be hanged thereon. (v. 14.)

They hanged Haman on the gallows that he had prepared for Mordecai. (vii. 10.)

JOB.

Oxen, asses, sheep, camels, sons and daughters . . . all destroyed. (i. 14-19.)

The Lord gave Job twice as much as he had before. . . . Sheep, camels, oxen, asses, sons and daughters. (xlii. 10, 12, 13.)

PSALMS.

Mine iniquities are gone over mine head : as an heavy burden they are too heavy for me. (Ps. xxxviii. 4.)

Who forgiveth all thine iniquities . . . As far as the east is from the west, so far hath He removed our transgressions from us. (Ps. ciii. 3, 12.)

ECCLESIASTES.

A little city, and few men within it : and there came a great king against it, and besieged it. (ix. 14.)

There was found in it a poor wise man, and he by his wisdom delivered the city. (ix. 15.)

SONG OF SOLOMON.

I sought Him, but I found Him not. (iii. 1.)

I found Him whom my soul loveth. (iii. 4.)

My Beloved had withdrawn Himself, and was gone. (v. 6.)

Who is this that cometh up from the wilderness, leaning upon her Beloved ? (viii. 5.)

ISAIAH.

I am a man of unclean lips. (vi. 5.)

Thine iniquity is taken away, and thy sin is purged. (vi. 7.)

Thou wast angry with me. (xii. 1.)

Thine anger is turned away. (xii. 1.)

THE STONE ROLLED AWAY.

ISAIAH—continued.

All . . . gone astray . . . turned every one to his own way. (liii. 6.)

The Lord hath laid on Him the iniquity of us all. (liii. 6.)

Broken-hearted . . . captives . . . them that are bound . . . ashes . . . mourning . . . the spirit of heaviness (lxi. 1, 3.)

Bound up . . . liberty proclaimed . . . the prison opened. Beauty . . . the oil of joy . . . the garment of praise. (lxi. 1, 3, with 10.)

JEREMIAH.

They took Jeremiah, and cast him into the dungeon. . . . And in the dungeon there was no water, but mire: so Jeremiah sunk in the mire. (xxxviii. 6.)

They drew up Jeremiah with cords, and took him up out of the dungeon. (xxxviii. 13.)

LAMENTATIONS.

He hath . . . brought me into darkness. . . . Surely against me is He turned. (iii. 2, 3.)

Thou drewest near . . . thou saidst, Fear not. O Lord, thou hast redeemed my life. (iii. 57, 58.)

EZEKIEL.

The soul that sinneth, it shall die. (xviii. 4, 20.)

Whosoever liveth, and believeth in Me shall never die. (John xi. 26.)

DANIEL.

Daniel requested that he might not defile himself by eating the king's meat. (i. 8.)

Melzar took away the portion of their meat. (i. 16.)

They sought Daniel . . . to be slain. (ii. 13.)

The king made Daniel a great man. (ii. 48.)

These men were bound . . . and were cast into the midst of the burning fiery furnace. (iii. 21.)

The king promoted Shadrach, Meshach, and Abednego in the province of Babylon. (iii. 30.)

THE STONE ROLLED AWAY.

DANIEL—continued.

They brought Daniel, and cast him into the den of lions. (vi. 16.)

Daniel was taken up out of the den, and no manner of hurt was found upon him. (vi. 23.)

There remained no strength in me. (x. 8.)

When He had spoken unto me, I was strengthened. (x. 19.)

HOSEA.

Ephraim is joined to idols: let him alone. (iv. 17.)

I will heal their backsliding, I will love them freely. . . . Ephraim shall say, What have I to do any more with idols? (xiv. 4, 8.)

JONAH.

There was a mighty tempest in the sea. (i. 4.)

The sea ceased from her raging. (i. 15.)

Jonah prayed unto the Lord . . . out of the fish's belly. (ii. 1.)

The fish vomited out Jonah upon the dry land. (ii. 10.)

Yet forty days, and Nineveh shall be overthrown. (iii. 4.)

God repented of the evil . . . and He did it not. (iii. 10.)

HAGGAI.

Mine house . . . is waste. (i. 19.)

The glory of this latter house . . . greater than of the former. (ii. 9.)

The heaven over you is stayed from dew, and the earth is stayed from her fruit. (i. 10.)

From this day will I bless you. (ii. 19.)

ZECHARIAH.

Joshua was clothed with filthy garments. (iii. 3.)

They set a fair mitre upon his head . . . and clothed him with garments. (iii. 5.)

O great mountain. (iv. 7.)

A plain. (iv. 7.)

THE STONE ROLLED AWAY.

MATTHEW.

Herod will seek the young child to destroy him. (ii. 13.)

Joseph took the young child and his mother, and departed into Egypt. (ii. 14.)

Jesus was led up of the spirit into the wilderness to be tempted of the devil. (iv. 1.)

Behold, there came a leper. (viii. 2.)

My servant lieth at home sick of the palsy. (viii. 6.)

Peter's wife's mother laid sick of a fever. (viii. 14.)

Many possessed with devils. (viii. 16.)

Then there arose a great tempest. (viii. 24.)

A man sick of the palsy, lying on a bed. (ix. 2.)

My daughter is even now dead. (ix. 18.)

A woman with an issue of blood twelve years. (ix. 20.)

Two blind men followed Him. (ix. 27.)

A dumb man possessed with a devil. (ix. 32.)

He departed until the death of Herod. (ii. 14, 15.)

He arose, and took the young child and his mother, and came into the land of Israel. (ii. 21.)

The devil leaveth Him. (iv. 11.)

And immediately his leprosy was cleansed. (viii. 3.)

The servant was healed in the self-same hour. (viii. 13.)

The fever left her. (viii. 15.)

He cast out the spirits. (viii. 16.)

There was a great calm. (viii. 26.)

He arose, and departed to his house. (ix. 7.)

The maid arose. (ix. 25.)

The woman was made whole from that very hour. (ix. 22.)

Their eyes were opened. (ix. 30.)

The devil was cast out, and the dumb spake. (ix. 33.)

THE STONE   ROLLED AWAY,

MATTHEW—continued.

A man which had his hand withered. (xii. 10.)	Restored whole, like as the other. (xii. 13.)
One possessed with a devil, blind, and dumb, was brought to Him. (xii. 22.)	The blind and dumb both spake and saw. (xii. 22.)
The wind was contrary. (xiv. 24.)	The wind ceased. (xiv. 32.)
It is a spirit. (xiv. 26.)	It is I. (xiv. 27.)
Peter began to sink. (xiv. 30.)	Jesus caught him. (xiv. 31.)
All that were diseased. (xiv. 35.)	Were made perfectly whole. (xiv. 36.)
My daughter is grievously vexed with a devil. (xv. 22.)	Her daughter was made whole from that very hour. (xv. 28.)
Lame, blind, dumb, maimed. (xv. 30.)	He healed them. (xv. 30.)
They have nothing to eat. (xv. 32.)	They did all eat, and were filled. (xv. 37.)
He is lunatic, and sore vexed. (xvii. 15.)	The child was cured from that very hour. (xvii. 18.)
Two blind men sitting by the way side. (Matt. xx. 30.)	Immediately their eyes received sight, and they followed Him. (xx. 34.)
He rolled a great stone to the door of the sepulchre. (xxvii. 60.)	The angel of God came and rolled back the stone from the door. (xxviii. 2.)
Jesus yielded up the ghost. (xxvii. 50.)	Jesus met them, saying, All hail. Lo, I am with you alway, even unto the end of the world. (xxviii. 9–20.)

THE STONE ROLLED AWAY.

MARK.

There was a man in the synagogue with an unclean spirit. (i. 23.)

He came out of him. (i. 26.)

One that was deaf, &c. (vii. 32.)

Straightway his ears were opened. (vii. 35.)

They bring a blind man unto Him. (viii. 22.)

He was restored, and saw every man clearly. (viii. 25.)

Women looking on afar off ... Mary beheld where he was laid. (xv. 40, 47.)

He appeared first to Mary Magdalene. (xvi. 9.)

LUKE.

They (Elisabeth & Zechariah) had no child. (i. 7.)

She brought forth a son. (i. 57.)

Simeon was waiting for the consolation of Israel. (ii. 25.)

Mine eyes have seen thy salvation. (ii. 30.)

They turned back ... seeking Him. (ii. 45.)

After three days they found Him. (ii. 46.)

We have toiled all night, and taken nothing. (v. 5.)

They inclosed a great multitude of fishes. (v. 6, 7.)

A great multitude of people came to be healed. (vi. 17.)

And they were healed. (vi. 18.)

A dead man carried out, the only son of his mother. (vii. 12.)

He that was dead sat up, and began to speak. (vii. 15.)

A woman in the city, which was a sinner. (vii. 37.)

Her sins, which are many, are forgiven. (vii. 47.)

A man, which had devils long time, and ware no clothes. (viii. 27.)

Then went the devils out of the man ... clothed. (viii. 33, 35.)

THE STONE ROLLED AWAY,

LUKE—continued.

A spirit taketh him. (ix. 39.)

Jesus healed the child. (ix. 42.)

A woman who had a spirit of infirmity eighteen years. (xiii. 11.)

Immediately she was made straight. (xiii. 13.)

A certain man which had the dropsy. (xiv. 2.)

He took him, and healed him. (xiv. 4.)

Ten men which were lepers. (xvii. 12.)

He said, Go shew yourselves to the priest. As they went they were cleansed. (xvii. 14.)

He sought to see Jesus, and could not. (xix. 3.)

To-day I must abide at thy house. (xix. 5.)

Smote off his ear. (xxii. 50.)

He touched his ear, and healed him. (xxii. 51.)

We receive the due reward of our deeds. (xxii. 41.)

To-day shalt thou be with me in paradise. (xxii. 43.)

A great company of people, and of women ... bewailed and lamented Him. (xxiii. 27.)

They worshipped Him, and returned to Jerusalem with great joy. (xxiv. 52.)

Their eyes were holden that they should not know Him. (xxiv. 16.)

Their eyes were opened, and they knew Him. (xxiv. 31.)

JOHN.

They have no wine. (ii. 3.)

The water was made wine. (ii. 9.)

He was at the point of death. (iv. 47.)

Thy son liveth. (iv. 50.)

A certain man which had an infirmity thirty-eight years. (v. 5.)

Immediately the man was made whole. (v. 9.)

A man blind from his birth. (ix. 1.)

He washed, and came seeing. (ix. 7.)

THE STONE ROLLED AWAY.

JOHN—continued.

They cast him out. (ix. 34.)	Jesus found him. (ix. 35.)
Lazarus is dead. (xi. 14.)	He that was dead came forth. (xi. 44.)
They have taken away my Lord, and I know not where they have laid Him. (xx. 13.)	Jesus said unto her, Mary. (xx. 16.)
I will not believe. (xx. 25.)	My Lord and my God. (xx. 28.)
They caught nothing. (xxi. 3.)	They were not able to draw it for the multitude of fishes. (xxi. 6.)

ACTS.

A certain man lame from his mother's womb. (iii. 2.)	Immediately his feet and ancle-bones received strength. (iii. 7.)
They put them in the common prison. (v. 18.)	The angel opened the doors, and brought them forth. (v. 19.)
As for Saul, he made havoc of the church. (viii. 3.)	He preached Christ . . . that He is the Son of God. (ix. 20.)
How can I, except some man should guide me? (viii. 31.)	Then Philip preached unto him Jesus. (viii. 35.)
He saw no man. (ix. 8.)	He received sight. (ix. 18.)
They watched the gates day and night. (ix. 24.)	The disciples took him by night, and let him down by the wall in a basket. (ix. 25.)
A certain man, Æneas, which had kept his bed eight years. (ix. 33.)	He arose immediately. (ix. 34.)
Tabitha was sick and died. (ix. 37.)	She opened her eyes . . . and she sat up. (ix. 40.)

THE STONE ROLLED AWAY.

ACTS—continued.

Peter doubted in himself what this vision should mean. (x. 17.)

The Spirit said ... Arise ... and go ... doubting nothing. (x. 19, 20.)

Peter was kept in prison. (xii. 5.)

Peter stood before the gate. (xii. 14.)

Herod stretched forth his hand to vex certain of the Church. (xii. 1.)

The angel of the Lord smote him, and he was eaten of worms, and gave up the ghost. (xii. 23.)

Elymas the sorcerer withstood them. (xiii. 8.)

There fell on him a mist and darkness. (xiii. 11.)

A certain man impotent in his feet. (xiv. 8.)

He leaped and walked. (xiv. 10.)

They stoned Paul ... supposing him dead. (xiv. 19.)

He rose up, and came into the city. (xiv. 20.)

A certain damsel possessed with a spirit of divination. (xvi. 16.)

He came out the same hour. (xvi. 18.)

He made their feet fast in the stocks. (xvi. 24.)

Everyone's bands were loosed. (xvi. 26.)

He drew his sword, and would have killed himself. (xvi. 27.)

He rejoiced, believing in God with all his house. (xvi. 34.)

He thrust them into the inner prison. (xvi. 24.)

They went out of the prison. (xvi. 40.)

Eutychus was taken up dead. (xx. 9.)

They brought the young man alive. (xx. 12.)

The Jews banded together that they would neither eat nor drink till they had killed Paul. (xxiii. 12.)

The soldiers took Paul, and brought him by night to Antipatris. (xxiii. 31.)

THE STONE ROLLED AWAY.

ACTS—continued.

All hope that we should be saved was taken away. (xxvii. 20.)

They escaped all safe to land. (xxvii. 44.)

A viper fastened on Paul's hand. (xxviii. 3.)

He shook it off into the fire, and felt no harm. (xxviii. 5.)

Publius was sick of a fever and a bloody flux. (xxviii. 8.)

He healed him. (xxviii. 8.)

No man stood with me. (2 Tim. iv. 16.)

Notwithstanding the Lord stood with me. (2 Tim. iv. 17.)